Urban Development Futures in the San Joaquin Valley

• • •

Michael B. Teitz

Charles Dietzel

William Fulton

2005

Library of Congress Cataloging-in-Publication Data

Teitz, Michael B.

Urban development futures in the San Joaquin Valley / Michael B. Teitz.

p. cm.

Includes bibliographical references.

ISBN: 1-58213-092-2

1. Land use, Urban—California—San Joaquin Valley. 2. City planning—California—San Joaquin Valley. 3. Urbanization—California—San Joaquin Valley. 4. Land use—Government policy—California—San Joaquin Valley. I. Dietzel, Charles. II. Fulton, William B., 1955- III. Title.

HD266.C22S237 2004

333.77'15'097948—dc22

2004028025

Foreword

It is generally agreed that California's inland areas, with their ample supplies of water and developable land, will experience substantial urban growth in coming decades. The nature and intensity of their growing pains, however, remain unclear. Interstate 5 and Highway 99 are already jammed with traffic, and the state's continued budget crisis makes new construction problematic. Conflicts between urban growth and agricultural interests seem very likely, but how those conflicts will shape the region's future is uncertain. There is room for error—both literally and figuratively—when it comes to development in these inland areas, but if that growth is mishandled, the entire state will suffer. In this sense, these areas are key regions for maintaining California's golden dream into the 21st century.

Michael Teitz, Charles Dietzel, and William Fulton understood this challenge when they began their study, *Urban Development Futures in the San Joaquin Valley.* Using a sophisticated computer model to simulate urban growth in the San Joaquin Valley, they produced maps under four policy scenarios—accommodating urban development, prime farmland conservation, high-speed rail, and automobile-oriented managed growth. Their maps are not predictions so much as illustrations of possible outcomes, but taken together, they suggest that at least one million acres (much of it farmland) will be transferred to urban use by the year 2040 and that the density of urban development will decline as families continue to demand more detached single-family housing.

One is left with the impression that even with substantial urbanization, there will still be plenty of land available for multiple purposes.

Most important, the authors conclude that the future of the San Joaquin Valley is still very much in the hands of local governments. The Valley's eight counties and 62 cities have made most of the key land-use decisions independently, and they are unlikely to relinquish this power eagerly in coming years. These growth scenarios, however, show that public policy can and will make a difference in the location and consequences of development. They also indicate that some level of regional coordination could mitigate its less desirable outcomes. By making the future a little easier to visualize and understand, this report should stimulate public discussion about what makes sense for the region, its residents, and the state.

David W. Lyon
President and CEO
Public Policy Institute of California

Summary

In all likelihood, the population of California will grow from its current level of some 35 million people to somewhere between 45 million and 55 million by 2040. Where will these new millions live? Many will be accommodated in the crowded metropolitan coastal areas or in Southern California's Inland Empire. However, growth and development in those regions are increasingly resisted in the name of the environment and quality of life, despite the burden of high housing prices. Thus, these areas find it increasingly difficult to accommodate new development. Despite economic pressures to grow, the combination of rising costs and local opposition is likely to push a substantial number of people to seek homes and employment elsewhere.

The San Joaquin Valley is a likely outlet for this population pressure; with a youthful population, it is also a major source of growth in its own right from natural increase and immigration. At the outset of the 21st century, the San Joaquin Valley stands on the threshold of the second great transformation in the 150 years of its settlement by Mexicans and Americans. When it was first settled after the Gold Rush, the Valley was rapidly transformed into a great agricultural region, perhaps the richest in the world for its size. Now with forecasts of population growth that would double its population in the next 40 years from 3.3 million to over seven million, the Valley faces urbanization on an unprecedented scale.

This study explores the likely scale and extent of urban growth in the San Joaquin Valley over the next four decades. It is intended to help policymakers and the public assess the significance and implications of growth and to consider whether policy changes are merited. Our objective is to estimate the size and pattern of the urban growth that is likely to occur in the Valley between now and 2040. We also forecast how that pattern might change as a result of varying public policy scenarios. We employ a complex model that permits us to project urban growth, both its scale and location, and to consider the potential effects of changes in factors that affect urban growth. This model is not directly based on population growth; rather, it simulates the growth of the physical extent of urban areas using their historic patterns of development and rates of growth.

Future Valleys

With this model, we look at four broad scenarios for urban growth in the San Joaquin Valley out to 2040.

1. The Accommodating Urban Development scenario assumes that the underlying urbanization patterns of the last 60 years will continue 40 years into the future. It posits no significant regional constraints on urban growth beyond those implicit in the historic pattern of development, with its high level of infrastructure provision and ample resources, such as water. This scenario makes no explicit assumptions about specific transportation investments or availability of water, but it does implicitly assume that accessibility levels and water supplies would be adequate to permit development in a form similar to the one that has historically occurred.

2. The Prime Farmland Conservation scenario permits urbanization to continue following the historical pattern, but it prohibits urbanization of all 3.2 million acres of "prime farmland" in the San Joaquin Valley. It is unlikely that regulation of development at this scale could occur in the Valley, but as a scenario it provides a clear case that reflects the real and widely felt concern for farmland preservation.

3. The High-Speed Rail scenario reflects proposals currently under consideration for a high-speed rail system that would connect the Bay Area and Sacramento to Los Angeles, via the San Joaquin Valley. Under this scenario, the model increases the probability of urbanization within a 20-mile radius of the stations tentatively identified as part of the proposed high-speed

rail network and decreases the relative probability of urbanization outside that 20-mile radius.

4. The Automobile-Oriented Managed Growth scenario assumes that parts of Highway 65, a north-south highway on the eastern side of the Valley would be built; that several east-west routes would be improved; and that the probability of new development would be greater along these transportation corridors and along Interstate 5. Thus, this scenario suggests a future in which highway transportation improvements are made in the context of an effort to shape urban growth.

Although these scenarios are broad-brush in nature, they do bring out the likely features of future urban growth in the Valley. Continuation of previous trends in development, exemplified by the Accommodating Urban Development scenario, projects a future in which urban areas grow much faster than population, with major loss of farmland. With the likely population forecast for the time period, it would imply much lower gross urban population densities. The map of urbanized areas in 2040 shows major growth in the three northern counties, around Fresno, and around Bakersfield. U.S. Route 99 has almost continuous urban development, and there is considerable growth along Interstate 5. The Prime Farmland Conservation scenario, although unrealistic, still projects substantial urbanization and farmland loss, with urban densities little changed. Because of the location of prime farmland, development shifts onto land of other categories. The High-Speed Rail and Automobile-Oriented Managed Growth scenarios both envisage high levels of urbanization and farmland loss, although in somewhat different places, and with falling imputed urban population densities. The former tends to concentrate development around cities with rail stations; the latter restrains development, while preserving a strongly automobile-based form.

It is best to view these scenarios not as literal forecasts or predictions of what will occur but rather as conditional projections that permit useful comparisons. Nonetheless, some conclusions may be drawn.

First, if the future is anything like the past, the San Joaquin Valley will continue to urbanize a large amount of land to accommodate growth. Three of the four scenarios predicted urbanization of an additional one million acres of land or more by 2040—in essence, a tripling in the amount of urbanized land to accommodate new development. Because most such development occurs along highways, the perception of urbanization may be even greater than its reality.

Second, although the model used to project future development does not directly forecast population and density, if we use it in conjunction with separate population forecasts, it implies that the density of new development would decline. This is not surprising given the nature of the San Joaquin Valley, which is a vast plain consisting mostly of privately owned land, in a region where land prices are relatively low compared to those in the coastal metropolitan areas. The future urbanized parts of the San Joaquin Valley projected here would consist of automobile-oriented, low-rise development at lower-than-current gross densities.[1] This has significant implications for traffic congestion, air quality, and other side effects that we have not considered in this report.

One possible "brake" on the extent of urban expansion that the model does not address is the nature of California homebuilding practices. These practices, which originated in coastal locales such as the Bay Area and Orange County, tend to encourage relatively high-density, single-family development (six to eight units per acre). There are several reasons for this, among them high land cost; the costs of roads, water, and sewer systems, which, in California, are more likely to be borne by developers; and the economics of scale that have been perfected over a half-century of homebuilding. As a result, large-scale residential developers in California, unlike counterparts elsewhere in the country, rarely develop low-density projects. Although the San Joaquin Valley might differ in the future, experience in Sacramento, Phoenix, and other

---

[1] This does not necessarily imply lower densities in conventional housing subdivisions. Rather, it includes all urban uses, such as commercial and warehousing, which have been using more land over time, as well as the possibility of more scattered, very low-density housing of the type that has become prevalent in "exurban" development in the eastern and southern United States.

places where California homebuilders have exported their services suggest that they stick to familiar building practices wherever possible.

Third, urbanization in the forms projected in our scenarios implies that the amount of agricultural land in the San Joaquin Valley declines, perhaps dramatically. With the exception of the Prime Farmland Conservation scenario, which by definition protected all prime farmland from urbanization, all scenarios showed a decline in farmland of at least 15 percent. Even the Prime Farmland Conservation scenario showed a decline in farmland of almost 9 percent. In short, if urbanization pressure is as great as projected, it will be impossible to retain a good part of current farmland in the future. Such a decline does not necessarily imply an equivalent loss of agricultural income if farmers can increase the intensity of use on land that remains, but it does imply substantial pressure on water supplies, especially when combined with urban growth.

Fourth, clear tradeoffs can be identified between the different scenarios, and public policy could play a role in shaping the Valley's urban form depending on which policy goals are emphasized. For example, the prime farmland conservation scenario moves a significant amount of development away from prime farmland near existing population centers along Highway 99, distributing it throughout the Valley to locations where prime farmland does not exist but where farmland of statewide significance does exist. By contrast, the High-Speed Rail scenario focuses development along the Highway 99 corridor. Although that development is more concentrated and less patchy than in any other scenario, it also consumes a large amount of prime farmland near the existing cities. The Automobile-Oriented Managed Growth scenario locates development along highway corridors with the result that new development is automobile-dependent and at lower densities than currently exists in the region. But it consumes less land overall than the High-Speed Rail scenario, and it encroaches less on prime farmland, largely because the improved highways would attract development away from the core of prime farmland in the Valley.

All four scenarios are speculative and incomplete. Because many influences are not taken into account specifically in our model, what actually happens may be very different from these scenarios. But they do

illustrate the different directions growth might take, and they highlight
the kinds of choices the San Joaquin Valley will likely have to make to
assure a prosperous and livable future. Much will depend on policy
choices, especially by state and local governments.

Implications for Urban Development Policy

Urban growth is almost always incremental. Building a new city or
town from scratch is rare because it is costly and time-consuming,
although some successful attempts have been made, notably the City of
Irvine. More typically, growth takes the form mostly of additions to the
edges of existing places, along with the creation of a few new "growth
points" that start out small but may become large over time.
Incremental growth may not seem to create profound change, but over a
long period of time—such as 40 years—the effect can be dramatic. The
San Fernando Valley of 1970 bore little resemblance to that of 1930; the
Santa Clara Valley of 1990 was vastly different from that of 1950.
Change may occur in small increments, but ultimately a change in scale
of urbanization transforms the qualitative nature of places.

All urban growth is regulated to some degree, but the incremental
nature of urban growth in California is further compounded by the
fragmented nature of local government decisionmaking. In California,
virtually all land-use planning and permitting powers are delegated to
cities (inside their boundaries) and counties (in unincorporated areas).
Although these local governments must develop comprehensive land-use
planning efforts, they are not required to coordinate their efforts on a
regional or subregional level. Each city and county is permitted to
pursue its own land-use planning and permitting independently. There
are eight counties and 62 cities in the San Joaquin Valley, as well as a far
larger number of unincorporated places whose inhabitants have strong
interests in the welfare of their communities.

Many regional government structures do exist, mostly as a way to
implement state or federal law. All eight counties are included in the San
Joaquin Valley Air Quality Management District, which regulates
stationary sources of air pollution pursuant to the federal Clean Air Act.
Each county has its own Council of Governments, which engages in
transportation planning and also allocates the state's "target" for housing

production within each county under the Housing Element law. As elsewhere in California, some subregional coordination is achieved through special districts (especially irrigation districts in the San Joaquin Valley) and joint powers authorities. In addition, local governments in California can seek to influence each other's land-use plan through commenting—and sometimes suing—under the California Environmental Quality Act.

These mechanisms do offer some opportunities for regional coordination, but they do not enable the entire Valley to craft and implement regional policies affecting growth patterns. In practice, quite the opposite is true. Each city and county makes its own plans for future growth and then implements those plans—usually with little concern for the cumulative regional effect of their actions. Nonetheless, other cities, regions, and states have evolved a number of tools for managing urban growth.

What is the likelihood of citizen support for any kind of anticipatory regional response to future urbanization? The report concludes with a brief consideration of potential responses, based on an analysis of responses from PPIC Statewide Surveys over the past five years. It is evident that the Valley's residents like their communities and their style of life. However, they are also increasingly aware of serious problems, for example, air pollution and traffic congestion, associated with urbanization. Whether they are ready to address these issues through regional action is a harder question. Although they recognize the value of collaboration for regional solutions, they are loath to relinquish local control, and they strongly favor local ballot box decisionmaking. This ambivalence may make it difficult to respond to urbanization issues in a timely way. Nonetheless, the issue of development is stimulating debate and political mobilization. Whether that debate can shape future growth in time to offset some of its problems will become evident in the coming decades.

Contents

Foreword iii
Summary v
Figures xv
Tables xvii
Acknowledgments xxi

1. INTRODUCTION 1

2. GROWTH AND TRANSFORMATION IN THE SAN
   JOAQUIN VALLEY 9
   The First Transformation 9
   Urbanization in the San Joaquin Valley 12
   Social and Demographic Structure 16
   Economic Structure 19

3. URBANIZATION AND LAND-USE PATTERNS IN
   THE SAN JOAQUIN VALLEY 27
   Geographical Patterns of Urbanization in the Valley 27
   Distribution and Density of Population 30
   Existing Farmland 32
   Conclusion 33

4. URBANIZATION SCENARIOS FOR THE SAN
   JOAQUIN VALLEY 35
   Urban Development Scenarios 36
   Limitations of SLEUTH 41

5. FUTURE VALLEYS: RESULTS OF THE FOUR
   GROWTH SCENARIOS 45
   Overview of the Scenarios 45
   Accommodating Urban Development 48
   Prime Farmland Conservation 51
   High-Speed Rail 55
   Automobile-Oriented Managed Growth 59
   Conclusion 63

6. PUBLIC OPINION AND POLICY CHOICES FOR THE
   SAN JOAQUIN VALLEY........................... 67
   Issues in Urban Development 67
   Past and Current Regionalism Efforts in the San Joaquin
      Valley 69
   Growth Policy Options for the San Joaquin Valley 71
      Transportation Investments 72
      Conservation of Nonurbanized Land 73
      Land-Use Density 74
      Financial Inducements That Can Shape Growth Patterns .. 74
      Examples from Other Regions and Other States 75
   Awareness of Development Issues in the San Joaquin Valley .. 77
   Attitudes Toward Responsibility and Policy............... 80
   Conclusion 82

Appendix: The SLEUTH Model 85

References 109

About the Authors 113

Related PPIC Publications 115

Figures

1.1. Location of and Urbanization in the San Joaquin
      Valley   3
2.1. Population Growth in the San Joaquin Valley,
      1900–2000   13
2.2a. California Age Pyramid, 2000   17
2.2b. San Joaquin Valley Age Pyramid, 2000   17
3.1. San Joaquin Valley Land Use, 2000   28
3.2. Historical Urbanization of the San Joaquin Valley,
      1900–2000   29
3.3. Type of Farmland in the San Joaquin Valley, 2000   33
4.1. Proposed High-Speed Rail Route and Stops Assumed in
      the High-Speed Rail Scenario.   38
4.2. Improved Transportation Routes in the Automobile-
      Oriented Managed Growth Scenario.   39
5.1. Geographical Pattern of Urbanization Under the
      Accommodating Urban Development Scenario,
      2000–2040   48
5.2. Geographical Pattern of Urbanization Under the Prime
      Farmland Conservation Scenario, 2000–2040   52
5.3. Geographical Pattern of Urbanization Under the High-
      Speed Rail Scenario, 2000–2040   56
5.4. Geographical Pattern of Urbanization Under the
      Automobile-Oriented Managed Growth Scenario,
      2000–2040   60
A.1. Process of Spontaneous Growth and Pseudo Code   88
A.2. Process of New Spreading Centers   89
A.3. Process of Edge Growth   90
A.4. Steps in Road-Influenced Growth: Searching the Cell
      Neighborhood for the Transportation Network, Taking
      a Random Walk, Establishing a Temporary Spreading
      Center, and Finally Establishing Urban Growth   92
A.5. Growth Patterns Under the Self-Modification Rules   94

Tables

2.1.   Urban and Rural Population Growth in the San Joaquin
       Valley, 1970–2000 14
2.2.   Population Growth in Major Cities in the San Joaquin
       Valley, 1970–2000 15
2.3.   Percentage of Latino and Foreign-Born Population in the
       San Joaquin Valley and California, 2000 18
2.4.   Population Growth and Components of Change in the
       San Joaquin Valley, 1970–2000 18
2.5.   Persons per Household in the San Joaquin Valley,
       1970–2000 19
2.6.   San Joaquin Valley Employment, by Sector,
       1970–2000 20
2.7.   Per-Capita Income Rankings for the Top 10 California
       Counties, California, and San Joaquin Valley Counties,
       2000 22
2.8.   Percentage of Population Living Below Poverty in the
       San Joaquin Valley and California, 1970–2000 23
2.9.   Average Annual Earnings per Employee and Rankings
       for the Top 10 California Counties, California, and San
       Joaquin Valley Counties, 2000 24
2.10. Labor Force, Employment, and Unemployment Rates
       for the San Joaquin Valley and California, 2003 25
3.1.   Population, Urbanization, and Population Density in
       the San Joaquin Valley, 2000 30
3.2.   Type of Farmland in the San Joaquin Valley, 2000 32
4.1.   Projected Population Growth in the San Joaquin Valley,
       2000–2040 40
5.1.   Changes in Urbanized Land Acreage in the San Joaquin
       Valley Under Four Scenarios, 2000–2040 46
5.2.   Loss of Farmland Acreage in the San Joaquin Valley
       Under Four Scenarios, 2000–2040 47

5.3.   Urbanized Acreage in the San Joaquin Valley Under the Accommodating Urban Development Scenario, by County, 2000–2040 49

5.4.   Farmland Acreage Loss in the San Joaquin Valley Under the Accommodating Urban Development Scenario, 2000–2040 50

5.5.   Urbanized Acreage in the San Joaquin Valley Under the Prime Farmland Conservation Scenario, by County, 2000–2040 53

5.6.   Farmland Acreage Loss in the San Joaquin Valley Under the Prime Farmland Conservation Scenario 55

5.7.   Urbanized Acreage in the San Joaquin Valley Under the High-Speed Rail Scenario, by County, 2000–2040 57

5.8.   Farmland Acreage Loss in the San Joaquin Valley Under the High-Speed Rail Scenario, 2000–2040 59

5.9.   Urbanized Acreage in the San Joaquin Valley Under the Automobile-Oriented Managed Growth Scenario, by County, 2000–2040 61

5.10. Farmland Acreage Loss in the San Joaquin Valley Under the Automobile-Oriented Managed Growth Scenario, 2000–2040 63

6.1.   San Joaquin Valley Residents' Ratings of Their Communities as Places to Live, 1999–2004 78

6.2.   San Joaquin Valley Residents Seeing the Issue as a Big Problem, 1999–2004 79

A.1. Metrics That Can Be Used to Evaluate the Goodness of Fit of SLEUTH 95

A.2. Historical Sources of Data Used to Recreate the Urbanization of the San Joaquin Valley, 1940–2000 99

A.3. Routines and Results for Calibrating SLEUTH for Fresno County, 1960–2000 101

A.4. Routines and Results for Calibrating SLEUTH for Kern County, 1960–2000 102

A.5. Routines and Results for Calibrating SLEUTH for Kings County, 1960–2000 103

A.6. Routines and Results for Calibrating SLEUTH for Madera County, 1960–2000 104

A.7. Routines and Results for Calibrating SLEUTH for Merced County, 1960–2000 105

A.8. Routines and Results for Calibrating SLEUTH for San Joaquin County, 1960–2000 106

A.9. Routines and Results for Calibrating SLEUTH for Stanislaus County, 1960–2000 107

A.10. Routines and Results for Calibrating SLEUTH for Tulare County, 1960–2000 108

Acknowledgments

The authors gratefully acknowledge the help that they received from many people during the course of this project. Carol Whiteside, president of the Great Valley Center, provided her insight into the San Joaquin Valley and an opportunity to preview some of our results at the annual conference sponsored by the Great Valley Center. A number of people in the Valley gave us the benefit of their experience with development, especially Ron Freitas of the Stanislaus County Department of Planning and Community Development, Diane Guzman and Steve Brandt of the City of Visalia Community Development Department, George Finney of the Tulare County Association of Governments, and Keith Woodcock of the Tulare County Resource Management Agency. Professor Keith Clarke at the Department of Geography, University of California, Santa Barbara, developed the SLEUTH model, without which the simulations could not have been done. Jeff Hemphill of the same department was invaluable in constructing the maps. Mark Feller at the Rocky Mountain Mapping Center of the U.S. Geological Survey assisted in finding data and providing the computer resources necessary for the simulations. Professor Lyna Wiggins of Rutgers University generously shared her expertise in geographic information systems and urban development. Antonina Simeti was a most effective and enthusiastic research associate for the project, especially in data development.

Drafts of this report were intensively reviewed by Mark Baldassare, Ellen Hanak, Jon Haveman, Doug Henton of Collaborative Economics, Hans Johnson, Joyce Peterson, and Professor Al Sokolow of the University of California, Davis. The authors appreciate their incisive critiques and valuable suggestions for improvement. Peter Richardson edited the initial draft, much to its benefit. Finally, Lisa Cole and Madhavi Katikaneni provided admirable support for a complex project, and Vanessa Merina helped to bring the report to fruition. Of course, responsibility for any shortcomings in the report remains with the authors alone.

1. Introduction

California's population is projected to grow from its current level of some 35 million people to somewhere between 45 million and 55 million by 2040.[1] Much of this additional population will be accommodated in the crowded metropolitan coastal areas and in Southern California's Inland Empire. But these areas are finding it increasingly difficult to accommodate new development. Despite economic pressures to grow, the combination of rising costs and local opposition to growth is likely to push many people to seek homes and employment elsewhere. The San Joaquin Valley is a likely escape valve for this population pressure, as well as being a major source of growth in its own right from natural increase and immigration. As the focus of California's continuing growth shifts from coastal to inland areas, the San Joaquin Valley is beginning to undergo its greatest transformation since Mexican and American settlers began to farm it on a large scale in the 19th century.[2]

This study seeks to estimate the likely scale and extent of this growth and consequent urbanization in the San Joaquin Valley over the next four decades. This fundamental information is intended to help policymakers and the public assess the significance and implications of growth and to consider whether policy changes are merited.

---

[1]Population forecasts are necessarily uncertain. We have relied largely on forecasts by the California State Department of Finance and although those forecasts for 2040 have recently been downsized, current estimates suggest that the range given here is reasonable (Lee, Miller, and Edwards, 2003).

[2]The San Joaquin Valley as defined here comprises eight counties—San Joaquin, Stanislaus, Merced, Madera, Fresno, Tulare, Kings, and Kern. Geographically, it is the southern portion of the Central Valley of California, extending from the Sierra Nevada to the Coast Ranges. It includes the drainage of the San Joaquin River and the internal drainage of several rivers into the Tulare Basin. Under our definition, the San Joaquin Valley covers 27,000 square miles (see Figure 1.1, below).

Since the time of Mexican and American settlement, the San Joaquin Valley has been a predominantly agricultural region—albeit with a diverse and changing crop pattern over time. The Valley's population has also been growing rapidly over the last century—doubling approximately every 30 years since 1900. Even by California standards, the sheer volume of this population growth is significant. From 1900 to about 1970, population grew fairly steadily, from about 200,000 to 1.6 million. Between 1970 and 2000, however, the Valley added 1.7 million people, bringing the total population to 3.3 million. Demographers forecast that the Valley's population will double yet again—adding about four million more people—by 2040. This is the equivalent of adding 10 new Fresnos or putting the current population of Santa Clara, Alameda, and Contra Costa Counties into the eight-county San Joaquin Valley area.

This new population growth is likely to bring the most profound transformation that the San Joaquin Valley has ever seen. Even though it grew from 200,000 to three million people in the 20th century, the Valley underwent much less of a transformation than did the Bay Area and Southern California during the Great Depression, World War II, the Cold War, and other epic economic and demographic events. Amid all the population growth, the agricultural foundation of the Valley's economy—and the urban structure that agriculture created—did not fundamentally change.

Most of the Valley's population growth in the 20th century built on the region's transformation in the 19th century from a sparsely inhabited natural area to a center of large-scale agriculture. That earlier transformation saw a vast area of seasonal wetlands and waterways drained, fenced, and converted to farmland. At the same time, with the construction of railroads along a north-south axis at the eastern side of the Valley, a network of towns was built there to serve the agricultural economy.

Some of those settlements prospered and in the course of time became substantial cities—Stockton, Modesto, Fresno, and Bakersfield, as shown in Figure 1.1. Others served a more modest role, yet survived, defining a pattern of beads on the necklace of the railroads—and, today,

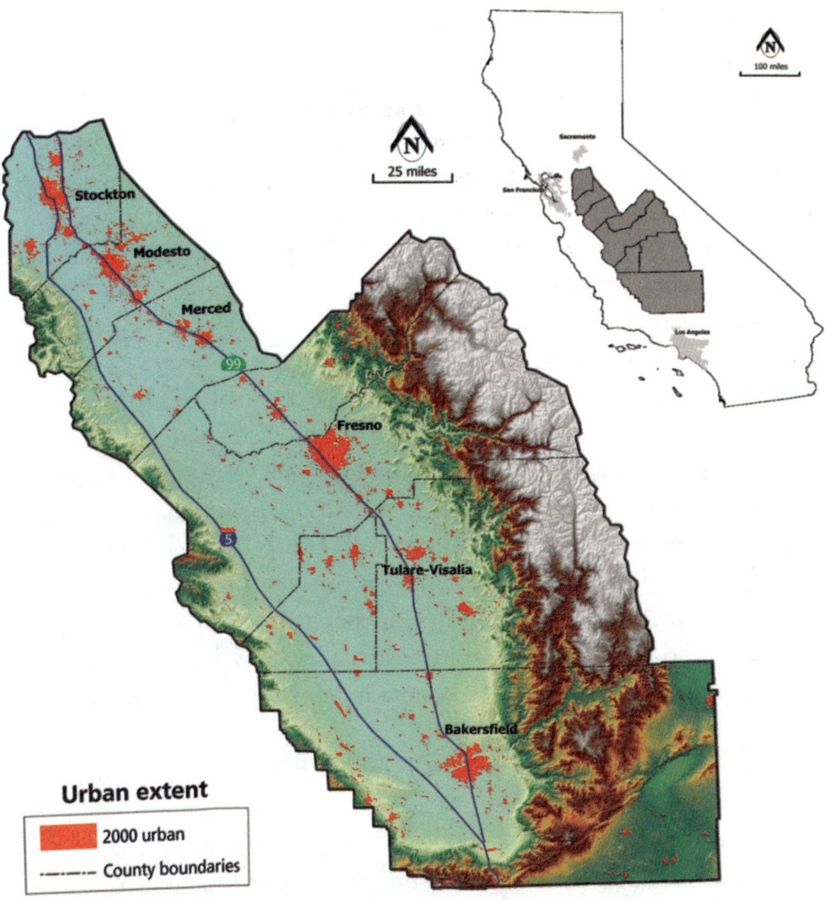

Figure 1.1—Location of and Urbanization in the San Joaquin Valley

Highway 99. As the Valley has grown to three million people, this basic pattern has become blurred, but it has not changed.

The Valley's future growth will almost certainly have a different character. Of the estimated four million new people expected in the next 40 years, fewer will be employed in agriculture, and they will live in urban areas that are largely yet to be built. Given the fact that people throughout the United States are living at lower densities than in the past, this additional population is likely to have an even greater effect on the landscape than their numbers would suggest. What will actually happen is far from clear.[3]

Urban growth is almost always incremental. Building a new city or new town from scratch is rare because it is costly and time-consuming, although some successful attempts have been made, notably the City of Irvine. More typically, growth occurs on the edges of existing places, along with the creation of a few new "growth points" that start out small but may become large over time.

The incremental nature of urban growth in California is further compounded by the fragmented nature of local government decisionmaking. In California, virtually all land-use planning and permitting powers are delegated to cities (inside their boundaries) and counties (in unincorporated areas). Although these local governments are required to engage in comprehensive land-use planning efforts, there is no requirement that they coordinate their efforts on a regional or subregional level. Each city and county is permitted to pursue its own land-use planning and permit efforts independently. There are eight counties and 62 cities in the San Joaquin Valley, as well as a far larger number of unincorporated places whose inhabitants have strong interests in the welfare of their communities.

Many regional government structures do exist, mostly as a way to implement state or federal law. All eight counties are included in the San Joaquin Valley Air Quality Management District, which regulates stationary, i.e., other than vehicle, sources of air pollution pursuant to the federal Clean Air Act. Each county has its own Council of Governments, which engages in transportation planning and also allocates the state's "target" for housing production within each county under the Housing Element law. Some subregional coordination is achieved through special districts (especially irrigation districts in the San Joaquin Valley) and joint powers authorities. In addition, local governments in California can seek to influence each other's land-use plans by commenting—and sometimes suing—under the California Environmental Quality Act (CEQA).

---

[3]Low-density growth is being actively opposed by proponents of "Smart Growth" and the "New Urbanism." This report does not advocate any specific development type.

Although these mechanisms provide some opportunities for regional coordination, they do not enable the entire Valley to craft and implement regional policies affecting growth patterns. In practice, quite the opposite is true. Each city and county makes its own plans for future growth and then implements those plans—usually with little concern for the cumulative regional effect of their actions.

Incremental growth may not seem to create profound change, but over a long period of time—such as 40 years—the effect can be dramatic. The San Fernando Valley of 1970 bore little resemblance to that of 1930; the Santa Clara Valley of 1990 was vastly different from that of 1950. Change may occur in small increments, but ultimately a change in scale of urbanization transforms the qualitative nature of places.

The San Joaquin Valley is far larger in area than those centers of urban growth mentioned above. Indeed, future urban growth in the San Joaquin Valley presents a different—and perhaps more profound— challenge. The Valley is huge, covering more than 27,000 square miles. Accommodating an additional four million people will almost certainly involve widespread development around many cities that are currently separated from each other but are nevertheless located on the same vast plain.

At first glance, adding four million people might not seem to require the consumption of large portions of this land. After all, the combined urbanized areas of San Francisco–Oakland–San Jose and Los Angeles– Riverside–San Bernardino—which together accommodate more than 20 million people—totaled only about 3,600 square miles in 1990, according to U.S. Census definitions.

However, the Census Bureau's definition of "urban" largely excludes much of what is now called exurban development—very low-density development that may have a rural feel but nonetheless transforms an area's character and use.[4] A more accurate measurement of urbanization based on housing density suggests that low-density exurban development

---

[4] Most discussions of density use U.S. Census definitions of urbanized areas. However, these definitions do not fully account for low-density patterns of development that have been occurring in much of the United States. Theobald (2001) constructs measures based on aggregations of census block groups.

is having a much greater effect on the American landscape. Even as the total amount of urban and suburban developed land in the United States grew in recent decades from about 73,000 square miles to 189,000 square miles, exurban development grew from 248,000 square miles to 591,000 square miles (Theobald, 2001).

This type of growth predominates in other parts of the country where land is inexpensive. Not only are people generally seeking larger houses and lots, but the entire apparatus of urban settlement—streets, commercial and industrial properties, public facilities, and other land uses—has become increasingly extensive. This means that for areas now on the urban frontier of growth, the footprint of development is much larger for a given population size. Such growth patterns are rare in coastal California. But on the vast canvas of the San Joaquin Valley—with its thousands of square miles of flat, privately owned, relatively inexpensive farmland—this development pattern could well occur over the next 40 years.

This report seeks to estimate the size and pattern of the urban growth that is likely to occur between now and 2040 and to forecast how that pattern might change as a result of different public policy scenarios. To do this, we employ a complex model that permits us to project urban growth, both its scale and location, and to consider the potential effects of changes in factors that affect that growth.

No model can tell us what the future will bring. Models can only spell out in a consistent way the logical consequences of our assumptions about the future, usually based on patterns observed in the past. But a good model also crystallizes the best of what we have learned about the forces that shape urban development. It will give us a projection that is internally consistent and not simple guesswork. Thus, its outputs form a basis against which we can test our knowledge and intuition, and its estimates of the effects of changes can shield us from wishful thinking.

Following this introduction, Chapter 2 provides a context for growth in California and the San Joaquin Valley, looking at the historical record. Chapter 3 describes the current urbanization pattern in the San Joaquin Valley. Chapter 4 introduces the four future scenarios we have constructed, drawing on an urban growth model that examines such possible influences as prime agricultural land preservation, the construction of new road and freeway links, or the development of a high-speed rail system. Chapter 5 discusses these scenarios in detail. Chapter 6 concludes by placing these scenario results in the context of future social and economic challenges for the San Joaquin Valley.

2. Growth and Transformation in the San Joaquin Valley

Beginning in the middle of the 19th century, the San Joaquin Valley experienced a transformation no less powerful than the one it faces now. That change also involved urbanization, but it was modest in its geographical extent. More important, urban growth was ancillary to the larger revolution that drove the transformation, namely, the adoption of large-scale agriculture in a region that was mostly in its natural state. The agriculture that produced this original transformation remains the foundation of the Valley's landscape and its social and economic systems today. Many of the challenges the Valley faces are embedded in the conflicts between the impending urbanization and the Valley's agricultural heritage—not only the agricultural landscape but also the economic and social structure created in that agricultural landscape.

The First Transformation

Up until the middle of the 19th century, the San Joaquin Valley—unlike the coastal areas of the state and the gold-laden Sierra foothills—remained in very much the same physical form as it had for millennia. Occupied by Native Americans, especially Yokuts and Miwoks, who lived by hunting, gathering, and modest cultivation, it was a vast bunchgrass prairie, interspersed with seasonal wetlands, riparian forest and Valley oak savanna, with dry saltbush in the south. In this regard, it bore little resemblance to the drained and leveled agricultural empires that emerged later. Much of what is now Kern County, for example, was a slough, and the Valley included two of the largest inland lakes in the United States—Tulare Lake in Kings County and Buena Vista Lake, near the bottom of the Grapevine close to present-day Interstate 5.

From the early 19th century, American trappers sought beaver, but there was little or no permanent European settlement.[1]

In the second half of the 19th century, the San Joaquin Valley was transformed—physically, economically, and socially—into an agricultural empire. Beginning in 1849, the Gold Rush dramatically changed both the growth dynamics of California and its wealth. As Carey McWilliams wrote in *California: The Great Exception*, by creating instant wealth, the Gold Rush allowed California to skip the typical agrarian homesteading phase of development that almost every other U.S. state experienced and to move directly to the creation of a sophisticated mercantile economy based on the accumulation of capital. This development, in turn, helped to create the rapid and dramatic transformation of the San Joaquin Valley into a large-scale agricultural region unlike most other farming areas of the United States.

Both federal and state policy encouraged small-scale homesteading in emerging agricultural areas such as the San Joaquin Valley, but these policies were soon overwhelmed by the state's wealth and the desire to use that wealth to kick-start large agricultural fortunes. The extension of the Central Pacific Railroad into the region in the 1870s hastened this trend. Despite bitter conflicts between the railroads and farmers, the new mode of transportation provided much cheaper, faster, and more reliable service to California markets and to the eastern United States. In so doing, it magnified the advantages of scale in agricultural production.

The Valley was an agricultural paradise with superb soils, plentiful water, and a hospitable climate, albeit hot in the summer. Almost anything could be grown, but available modes of transportation largely determined what would be grown and how far it could be shipped. Thus, it was no accident that grains of relatively high value, notably wheat, came first.[2] Farming was so strongly tied to transportation that in many cases the wheat fields stopped where the railroad line ended, and

---

[1]It is notable that no missions were established in the Valley, although efforts were made. The local inhabitants resisted incursions fiercely.

[2]It is also true that in some parts of the Valley, as elsewhere in California, there was also a period in which cattle hides were the dominant export.

were extended in conjunction with the railroad's expansion. Over time—with irrigation as well as access—production moved to higher-value crops requiring long-term capital investment, such as tree and row crops. Access to eastern markets and refrigeration meant that new, more intensively farmed products, such as fruit, could be grown profitably.

With continued in-migration after the Gold Rush boom had subsided, farmers experimented with new crops, creating a distinctive pattern of specialization and developing new products, such as raisins. They invested heavily in irrigation, turning to rivers flowing west from the Sierra Nevada and creating reliable flows and extensive water transportation systems. Through a process of social and technical learning and invention, they developed organizations to handle water—irrigation districts—and unique forms of agricultural equipment. And they prospered, albeit on the basis of a system of social relations that rapidly became class structured and, over time, based also on ethnicity, with Mexican immigrants doing the primary labor.

A half-century after the Gold Rush, the San Joaquin Valley had been physically, economically, and socially transformed. Where there had been prairie and wetlands, there were large and small farms, first cultivating wheat, then with irrigation, a continually changing pattern of tree and row crops. Where there had been many small, though interrelated Native American bands, there was death and dislocation, accompanied by an influx of European Americans. By 1900, within the memory of persons still living at the time, the Valley's landscape and society had been profoundly changed.

Although the original transformation took place in the late 19th century, these patterns continued well into the 20th century. Much large-scale farming began later on as a result of new irrigation projects. The construction of the federal Central Valley Project in the 1930s opened up more land for farming in the northern reaches of the San Joaquin Valley and permitted more irrigation-intensive crops. The construction of the State Water Project in the 1960s performed the same function for the southern Valley, especially Kern County.

Of course, agriculture was not the only source of income in the Valley. Over time, other activities proliferated, especially in the service sectors. However, perhaps the largest economic addition occurred with the discovery and exploitation of oil in the southern part of the Valley. It contributed substantially to the growth of Bakersfield and marked the area both socially and physically in ways that can still be seen today.

The result today is landscape transformation on a mammoth scale. Approximately 5.2 million acres of land are in agricultural cultivation in the San Joaquin Valley. For most natural landscape types, including wetlands, 90 percent or more of the original ecology has been lost. In the case of the bunchgrass prairie—once the predominant vegetation form on the San Joaquin Valley landscape—less than 1 percent remains today

Urbanization in the San Joaquin Valley

Urbanization also played an important role in the first transformation. Commercial agriculture required access to markets, whether in San Francisco or elsewhere in the world. The urbanization pattern that resulted from economic growth conformed largely to the needs of the agricultural economy for services and to the requirements of the transportation system.

Initially, small settlements grew up on waterways, although the intermittent river flows impeded large-scale transportation except at the northern end of the Valley. But the coming of the Central Pacific set in motion a much more powerful urbanization pattern. In response to the need for towns that would serve the agricultural economy, a string of small settlements grew along the railroad—in some instances also corresponding to earlier water transportation nodes. Often, they were likened to beads on a necklace. South from Sacramento, towns such as Lodi, Stockton, Modesto, Merced, Madera, Fresno, Visalia, Porterville, and Bakersfield became substantial places in their own right, with their own traditions and styles. But they were only the larger towns among the dozens that were scattered across the Valley, each serving its local area.

The Valley's nonnative population growth was not insignificant during the 19th century. Even as the original inhabitants were decimated, the population grew to 143,000 persons in 1900, or 9.6 percent of the state's total. As agriculture expanded in the 20th century, the population grew commensurately—barely slowing down in the aftermath of war or during economic depression.

Figure 2.1 shows the pattern of population growth over the 20th century. Although the rate of increase changes over the years, the overall impression is clearly one of striking absolute growth. The population tripled between 1900 and 1920, and it has grown rapidly ever since. Even in the depression of the 1930s, the Valley grew by over 35 percent, which was faster than in the 1920s. In good part, this may be attributable to migration from the Dust Bowl regions in Oklahoma and Arkansas—a migration commemorated in John Steinbeck's classic novel, *The Grapes of Wrath.* Under the stimulus of World War II, population accelerated again, growing by 55 percent in the 1940s.

Population growth was slowest during the 1960s, but even in that decade it increased by 15 percent. Since 1970, the Valley's population has grown rapidly again—increasing by at least 20 percent during each decade and doubling in 30 years. By 2000, the Valley's population was 3.3 million—23 times what it had been in 1900. Yet California's own population growth was also extraordinary during this period; the Valley simply kept pace with the state. At the turn of the 21st century, the

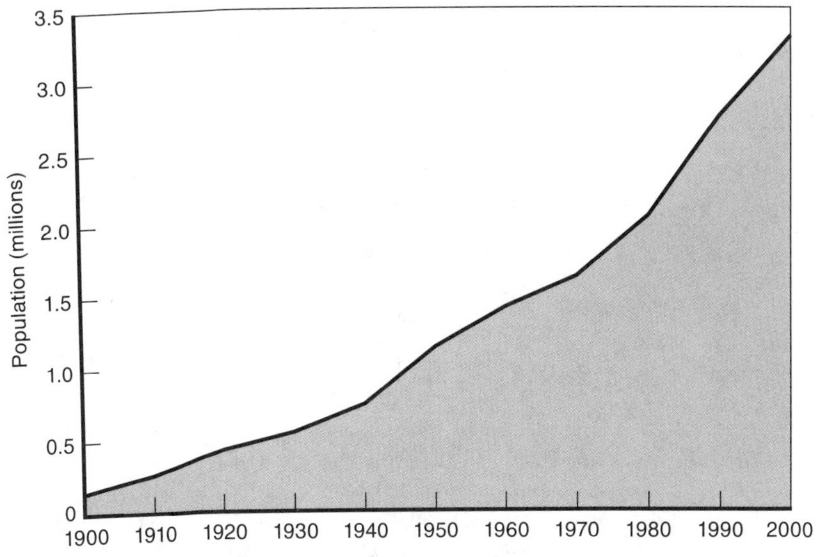

SOURCE: California Department of Finance Demographic Research Unit, 2003.

Figure 2.1—Population Growth in the San Joaquin Valley, 1900–2000

Valley's population was still 9.6 percent of the California total—exactly what it had been in 1900.

Given the fact that the San Joaquin Valley served as an agricultural region for the entire 20th century, it is perhaps surprising that the Valley's population is overwhelmingly urban and has been for some time (see Table 2.1). In 1990, the Census Bureau classified 81 percent of the San Joaquin Valley's population as urban—well below California's overall figure of 93 percent. By 2000, the urban population share for the San Joaquin Valley had increased to 87 percent, closing in on the state's figure of 94 percent. The rural farm population is an even smaller part of the total rural population. During the 1990s, it dropped from 2.6 percent to 1.6 percent. Even in absolute terms, the rural farm

Table 2.1

Urban and Rural Population Growth in the San Joaquin Valley, 1970–2000

	Population and Percentage of Total			
	1970	1980	1990	2000
North Valley	589,343	747,802	1,029,553	1,221,149
	100	100	100	100
Urban	411,814	584,972	865,986	1,089,436
	70	78	84	89
Rural	177,529	162,830	163,567	131,713
	30	22	16	11
South Valley	1,036,666	1,300,302	1,712,447	2,081,643
	100	100	100	100
Urban	732,308	965,857	1,343,184	1,775,326
	71	74	78	85
Rural	304,358	334,445	369,263	306,317
	29	26	22	15
Entire Valley	1,626,009	2,048,104	2,742,000	3,302,792
	100	100	100	100
Urban	1,144,122	1,550,829	2,209,170	2,864,762
	70	76	81	87
Rural	481,887	497,275	532,830	438,030
	30	24	19	13

SOURCE: U.S. Censuses, 1970–2000.

population declined, despite a large population increase Valley-wide. To some extent, this shift reflects changes in the way the U.S. Census Bureau counts urban and rural populations. However, it also shows quite clearly that the Valley's population is now overwhelmingly urban in character, although it is scattered among smaller cities with a decidedly rural style, rather than concentrated into one or two major metropolitan centers. According to recent surveys, this distinctive form of urbanization is one of the most favored features of Valley life among its inhabitants.

Table 2.1 also shows the rural-urban breakdown for the northern and southern San Joaquin Valley.[3] We will use this distinction in various parts of this report. It is useful in that northern counties are more connected to the San Francisco Bay Area and subject to direct spillovers of population and commuting, whereas the southern counties remain more rural and their cities more freestanding. However, in the extreme south, the influence of migration from the Los Angeles region is beginning to be felt.

To give some detail to this broad view of urbanization, Table 2.2 shows population growth in the five largest cities in the Valley. They account for about 36 percent of the total urban population, reinforcing the sense that urbanization in the Valley is not concentrated. However, they are growing faster than the population of the Valley as a whole.

Table 2.2

Population Growth in Major Cities in the San Joaquin Valley, 1970–2000

City	1970	1980	1990	2000
Fresno	165,972	217,346	354,091	427,652
Bakersfield	69,515	105,611	174,978	247,057
Stockton	109,963	149,779	210,943	243,771
Modesto	67,712	106,963	164,746	188,856
Visalia	27,268	49,729	75,659	91,565

SOURCE: U.S. Censuses, 1970–2000.

---

[3]The northern Valley is defined as the counties of San Joaquin, Stanislaus, and Merced; the southern Valley comprises Madera, Fresno, Tulare, Kings, and Kern Counties.

Between 1970 and 2000, a period during which the population of the San Joaquin Valley grew by 103 percent, the five cities combined grew from 440,000 people to 1.2 million people—an increase of 172 percent. By contrast, the rest of the Valley grew by 77 percent. Annexations undoubtedly also played a role in this growth but how much cannot be determined.

Social and Demographic Structure

Sheer population growth has been just one characteristic of change among many in the San Joaquin Valley in the last century. The region's large-scale agriculture has created a particular social and economic pattern characterized by a young population, relatively low educational attainment, and high poverty. Furthermore, as stated above, this population—which is largely derived from Valley residents who were originally farm workers—is now overwhelmingly urban. All of these trends have accelerated in the last 30 years, framing a new challenge as the Valley faces more urbanization in the 21st century.

Even though the scale of the Valley's population growth has mirrored that of California, the components of that population are significantly different. In particular, the Valley's population differs from the state's in age distribution and ethnicity. The Valley is much more heavily Latino than is the rest of the state, and it is much younger—characteristics that, again, derive in part from the fact that the historical population base was farm workers.

Figures 2a and 2b show the differences in the age profiles between the San Joaquin Valley and the state as a whole. The 2000 Census found that 35 percent of the Valley's population was under age 20, fully 5 percent more than the state. However, the Valley also showed a slightly smaller proportion in the older age groups—60 and over—with 13.5 percent as contrasted with 14 percent for the state. Thus, the Valley has a smaller proportion of its people in the prime working age groups and a substantially larger proportion of youth who must be nurtured and educated.

This difference is related to the Valley's ethnic composition and migrant population, with a higher proportion of Latinos (see Table 2.3),

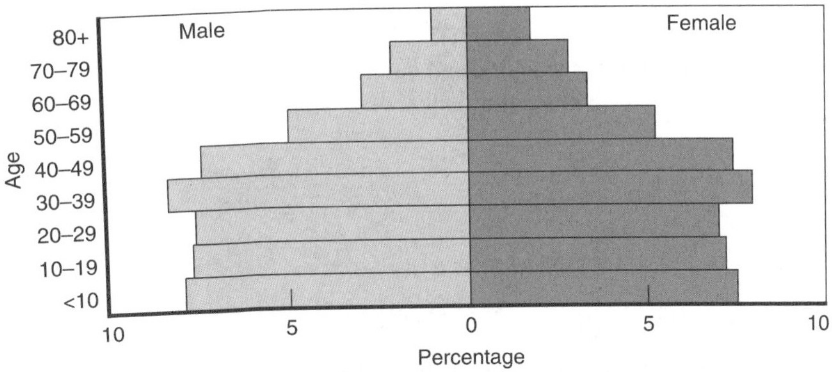

SOURCE: 2000 Census.

Figure 2.2a—California Age Pyramid, 2000

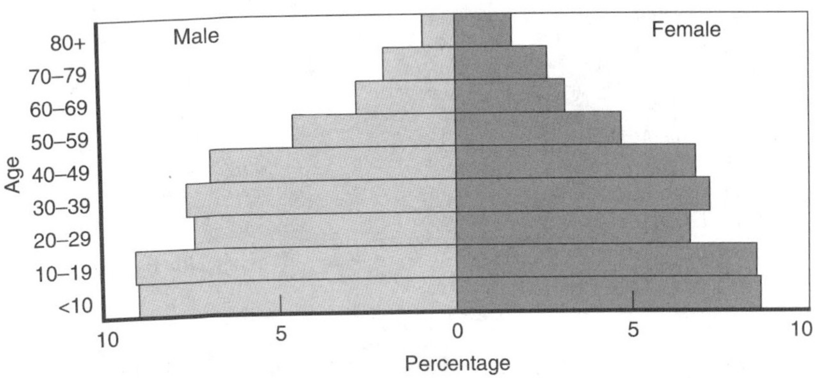

SOURCE: 2000 Census.

Figure 2.2b—San Joaquin Valley Age Pyramid, 2000

who tend to have larger households and higher birth rates. However, Table 2.3 also shows a lower proportion of persons born outside the United States, which may partially offset this tendency. These numbers also may not fully reflect the number of undocumented immigrants.

Table 2.4 reveals that net migration continues to account for a substantial part of the Valley's population growth. Although the

Table 2.3

**Percentage of Latino and Foreign-Born Population
in the San Joaquin Valley and California, 2000**

	Latino	Foreign-Born
San Joaquin Valley	39.8	19.8
California	32.4	26.2

SOURCE: U.S. 2000 Census.

Table 2.4

**Population Growth and Components of Change in the
San Joaquin Valley, 1970–2000**

Population Growth	North Valley	South Valley	Entire Valley
1970–1980	160,500	266,300	426,800
% natural increase	34	45	41
% net migration	66	55	59
1980–1990	281,500	412,700	694,200
% natural increase	37	48	44
% net migration	63	52	56
1990–2000	192,400	374,700	567,100
% natural increase	63	67	65
% net migration	37	33	35

SOURCE: California Department of Finance Demographic Research Unit, 2003.

proportion of growth from natural increase has risen substantially, net migration still provided over one-third of total growth in the 1990s.

Showing the effect of this demographic composition, household size in the Valley has remained higher than that of California as a whole (Table 2.5). At the same time, household size has rebounded in the last two decades after significant declines since the 1970s. Larger household sizes, together with limited income, may reduce future urbanization. Eventually, however, household size in the Valley may be expected to resume its decline, reflecting trends in the state and nation.

Table 2.5

**Persons per Household in the San Joaquin Valley,
1970–2000**

	1970	1980	1990	2000
North Valley	3.10	2.78	2.96	3.05
South Valley	3.21	2.87	2.99	3.11
Entire Valley	3.17	2.84	2.98	3.09
California	2.9	2.7	2.8	2.9

SOURCE: U.S. Censuses, 1970–2000.

Economic Structure

Even as the Valley's population evolves from its historical base of farmers and farm worker families, its economy is changing so that farming itself is now an important part of a much more diverse and complex economy.

Agriculture and related industries remain the backbone of the Valley's economy, although they are changing in character. Between 1970 and 2000, direct agricultural employment dropped from 15 percent of all Valley employment to only 8.4 percent. Most of this decline occurred between 1970 and 1990, when the number of farm jobs actually decreased. But indirectly, agriculture remains an important driver of the Valley's economy. Between 1970 and 2000, agricultural services employment quadrupled, growing from 4 percent to 8.5 percent of all jobs. Together, these two sectors accounted for 17 percent of total employment, compared with only 3 percent statewide. It may be that the influence of agriculture is greater still. Certainly, farming is visible everywhere in the Valley, and its cultural and political presence is equally strong. As revealed consistently by the PPIC Statewide Survey, the population strongly values its small town lifestyle, farmland, and open space.

Nonetheless, the economic structure of the Valley has been changing over time, reflecting the larger trends in the United States and the world. Table 2.6 shows that employment by industrial sector in the San Joaquin Valley has shifted in the decades from 1970 through 2000.[4] Over that

---

[4]Employment here includes both full- and part-time workers as well as proprietors.

Table 2.6

San Joaquin Valley Employment, by Sector, 1970–2000

Sector	Number of Employees and Percentage of Total Employment			
	1970	1980	1990	2000
Farm	107,217	115,180	105,204	132,271
	15.3	11.4	8.2	8.4
Agricultural services, forestry, fishing, and other	27,921	68,439	89,583	133,871
	4.0	6.8	7.0	8.5
Mining	8,330	14,292	17,087	11,456
	1.2	1.4	1.3	0.7
Construction	24,776	48,120	73,073	80,794
	3.5	4.8	5.7	5.2
Manufacturing	70,721	103,258	121,368	127,051
	10.1	10.2	9.4	8.1
Transportation and public utilities	33,449	44,467	51,997	67,172
	4.8	4.4	4.0	4.3
Wholesale trade	28,641	45,470	51,872	54,854
	4.1	4.5	4.0	3.5
Retail trade	107,340	152,492	201,945	241,845
	15.3	15.1	15.7	15.4
Finance, insurance, and real estate	39,456	64,841	78,333	92,421
	5.6	6.4	6.1	5.9
Services	113,065	181,489	276,749	378,263
	16.1	17.9	21.5	24.1
Government and government enter.	139,456	174,450	219,140	246,399
	19.9	17.2	17.0	15.7
Total employment	700,372	1,012,498	1,286,351	1,566,397
	100.0	100.0	100.0	100.0

SOURCE: Bureau of Economic Analysis Regional Economic Information System, 2003.

NOTE: Percentages may not sum to 100 because of rounding.

30-year period, the Valley saw its employment grow by 124 percent overall, slightly faster than that of the state. But the composition of its employment shifted in a similar way to that of the state and the nation, with a large absolute and relative increase in the service sector and a decline in the relative share in manufacturing—even as employment continued to grow.

Interestingly, the highly visible growth in warehousing and the Valley's role as a distribution center, both of which have been occurring in the past two decades, do not appear to be reflected in unusually high growth of employment in wholesale trade and transportation. Nonetheless, the rapid growth in logistics and warehousing is evident to observers and may be an important part of future economic development.[5]

Overall, the Valley has now become a diversified economy, although still deeply engaged with agriculture. The picture that emerges is consistent with the urban population growth described above, but how the economy will change with further growth remains unclear.

The downside of this economic structure is evident when we look at measures of income and poverty in the Valley (Table 2.7).

The figures are troubling. Not only does no Valley county equal or exceed the state average, but also of the eight counties, six rank among the lowest 13 in the state. This is not a high-wage region.

The picture of relative income deficiency suggested above is reinforced by federal government measures of poverty. The percentages of the population living in poverty in each county and the Valley, shown in Table 2.8, have not only exceeded those for California but appear to have become worse over the past two decades, after previously improving.

We should be careful not to infer that the low level of per-capita income in the Valley results solely because of its agricultural base. Table 2.9 shows average earnings per employee and county rank in the state for the eight Valley counties in 2000. Taking all sectors together, the Valley appears much less extreme by this measure. Despite the Valley's economic structure, its employees' earnings were not far out of line with earnings in other parts of the state outside the core metropolitan areas. On the other hand, county-by-county statistics across the state suggest that counties less dependent on agriculture have higher earnings per employee, which reflects, in part, the fact that these numbers include farm employees who are less likely to work year round.

---

[5]See Collaborative Economics (2000) for a review of the changing Valley economy and its opportunities.

Table 2.7

**Per-Capita Income Rankings for the Top 10 California
Counties, California, and San Joaquin Valley
Counties, 2000**

County	Income ($)	Rank
Top 10 California counties		
Marin	62,927	1
San Mateo	61,083	2
Santa Clara	55,677	3
San Francisco	55,182	4
Contra Costa	42,461	5
Alameda	38,525	6
Santa Cruz	37,866	7
Napa	37,788	8
Orange	35,446	9
Sonoma	35,193	10
California	32,363	—
San Joaquin Valley counties		
San Joaquin	23,212	35
Stanislaus	22,791	39
Fresno	21,265	46
Kern	20,543	47
Tulare	19,539	49
Madera	18,362	53
Merced	18,268	54
Kings	16,011	58

SOURCE: Bureau of Economic Analysis Regional
Economic Information System, 2003.

Although some wages are moderate or high, jobs remain scarce. In
2000, the year of our population and earnings data, the Valley's
unemployment was about 12.3 percent of the labor force—triple the
figure for California as a whole (Table 2.10). Furthermore, wage earners
making decent wages are often supporting many family members not in
the work force, thus dragging down per-capita income.

In sum, we find that agriculture has remained important to the
Valley's economic base but that actual farm employment is on the wane.
Agriculture's output increasingly involves new forms of production and a

Table 2.8

**Percentage of Population Living Below Poverty in the
San Joaquin Valley and California, 1970–2000**

County	1970	1980	1990	2000
Fresno	18.9	14.5	21.4	22.9
Kern	16.1	12.6	16.9	20.8
Kings	19.2	14.6	18.2	19.5
Madera	21.4	15.7	17.5	21.4
Merced	16.9	14.7	19.9	21.7
San Joaquin	14.4	13.3	15.7	17.7
Stanislaus	14.8	11.9	14.1	16.0
Tulare	19.3	16.5	22.6	23.9
Entire Valley	17.0	13.9	18.3	20.5
California	11.1	11.4	12.5	14.2

SOURCE: U.S. Censuses, 1970–2000.

more skilled labor force, similar to that in other sectors. The Valley's economy has diversified and is increasingly dominated by services. Meanwhile, the population has continued to grow, and this population is concentrated in urban areas. However, income levels remain far below statewide averages.

The picture that emerges is one of a region that continues to rely on a relatively low-paying and relatively low-value-added industry, agriculture, for much of its economic base and that has not yet found a way to integrate a rapidly growing population into a higher-paying urban economy. Whatever the causes, it appears that the Valley's economic structure will change with urbanization on a large scale, which leaves open the question of what kinds of economic activity and jobs will accompany future growth. Our analysis cannot answer that question, although it has been addressed elsewhere (Collaborative Economics, 2000). Rather, this report will throw into sharp relief the contrast implicit in the urbanization trends and the underlying social and economic structure. It is to those urbanization trends that we now turn.

Table 2.9

Average Annual Earnings per Employee and Rankings for the Top 10 California Counties, California, and San Joaquin Valley Counties, 2000

County	Earnings ($)	Rank
Top 10 California counties		
Santa Clara	73,749	1
San Mateo	65,693	2
San Francisco	61,714	3
Alameda	45,191	4
Contra Costa	43,243	5
Los Angeles	40,826	6
Marin	40,766	7
Orange	40,605	8
San Diego	38,990	9
Sacramento	38,972	10
California	41,651	—
San Joaquin Valley counties		
San Joaquin	31,450	23
Kern	31,075	24
Stanislaus	30,546	25
Kings	29,886	27
Fresno	28,632	35
Merced	27,664	38
Tulare	26,410	41
Madera	25,282	49

SOURCE: Bureau of Economic Analysis Regional Economic Information System, 2003.

Table 2.10

Labor Force, Employment, and Unemployment Rates for the San Joaquin Valley and California, 2003

County	Labor Force	Employed Population	Unemployment Rate
Fresno	390,600	334,600	14.3
Kern	287,100	254,700	11.3
Kings	45,830	39,440	13.9
Madera	54,600	48,200	11.8
Merced	84,510	72,260	14.5
San Joaquin	257,500	234,700	8.9
Stanislaus	204,300	182,900	10.5
Tulare	168,970	142,860	15.5
Entire Valley	1,493,410	1,309,660	12.3
California	16,884,200	16,048,900	4.9

SOURCE: Cálifornia Employment Development Department, 2003.

3. Urbanization and Land-Use Patterns in the San Joaquin Valley

The emergence of a regional economy based on agriculture—as well as the population growth and urbanization that accompanied that transformation—has left in its wake a distinctive land-use pattern that forms the template of the San Joaquin Valley today.

The eight counties of the San Joaquin Valley contain about 17.5 million acres of land, or about 27,300 square miles. As of 2000, about 5.7 million acres, or approximately 30 percent, were in agricultural production, including about 3.2 million acres classified by the state as "prime farmland." Approximately 600,000 acres, or about 3 percent, had been urbanized. The remaining 11 million or so acres of land were either barren, under water, or covered with something other than agricultural crops or urban use. A large portion of this land consisted of forest and similar land cover in the foothill areas of some of the counties, with a part of that in federal or other public lands. Figure 3.1 depicts the distribution of land uses in the eight-county area as of 2000.

Geographical Patterns of Urbanization in the Valley

That the urbanized area of the San Joaquin has grown rapidly in the last century, and especially in the last 25 years, is clear from Figure 3.2. Most of the growth has occurred adjacent to the agricultural towns that emerged along Highway 99 in the late 19th and early 20th centuries. Cities such as Modesto, Fresno, and Bakersfield have become major urban centers, with between 100,000 and 400,000 residents. Metropolitan Fresno now approaches one million people.

The geographical patterns within the Valley are important, especially in the context of the subregional economic differences noted above. The

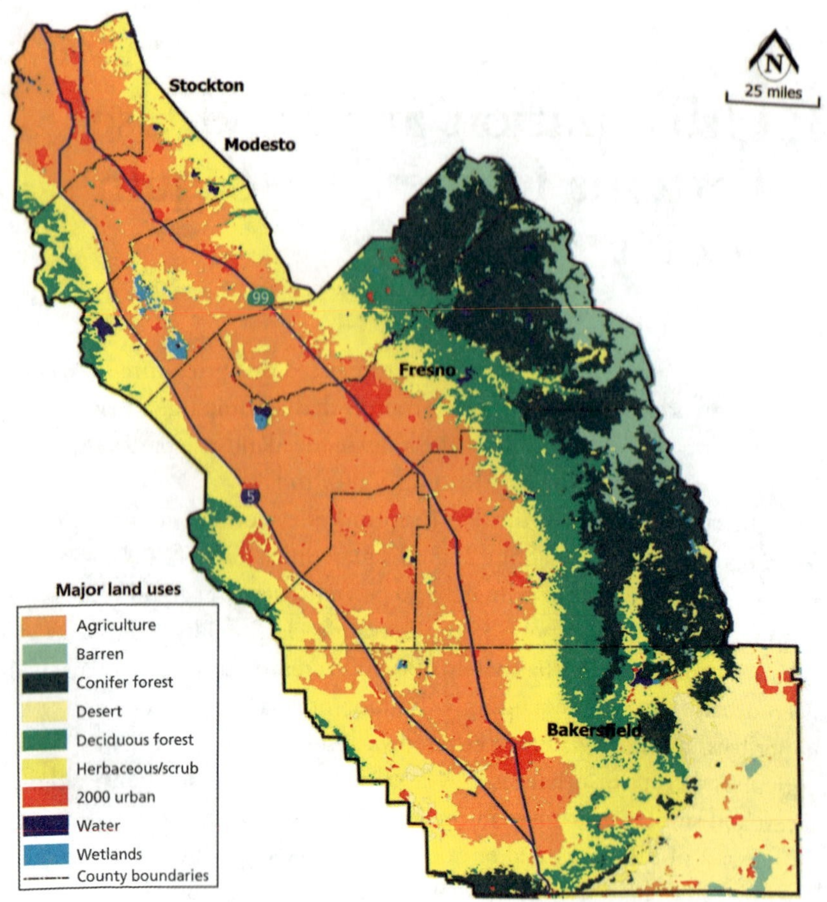

Figure 3.1—San Joaquin Valley Land Use, 2000

three northern counties—including the more affluent San Joaquin and Stanislaus Counties, which are influenced by the Bay Area—already show an almost continuous pattern of urbanization along Highway 99, with an extension to the west toward the Livermore Valley and the Bay Area along I-580. To the east, urbanization is also spreading from Modesto toward the Sierra Nevada foothills.

Farther south, in the agricultural heartland, Fresno remains the dominant center, with very substantial growth north and east from its

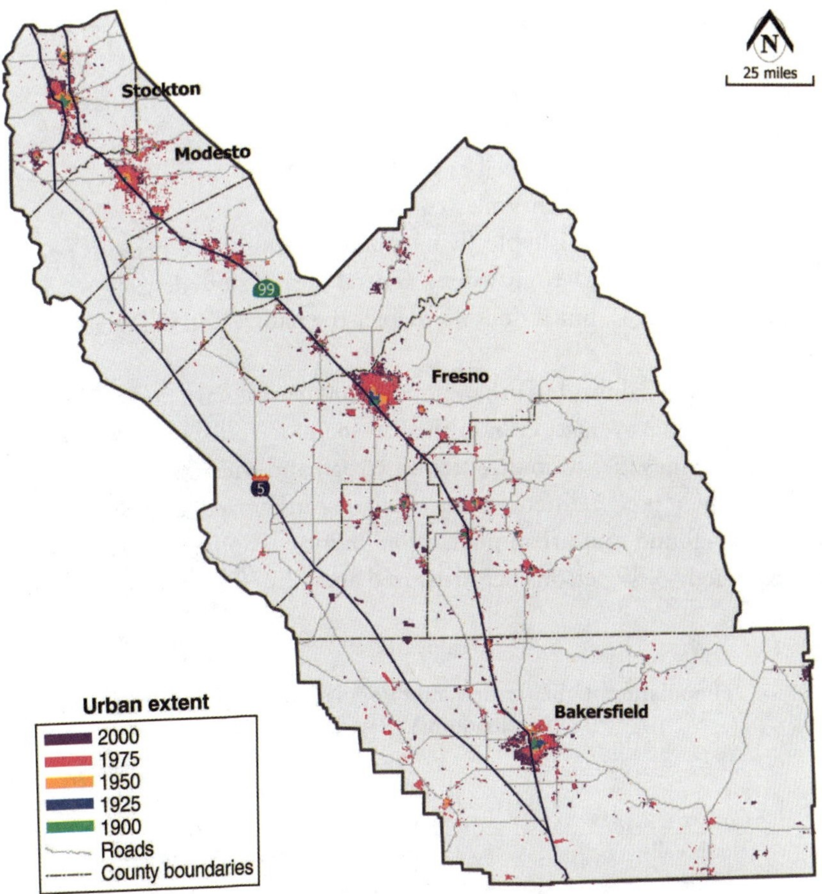

Figure 3.2—Historical Urbanization of the San Joaquin Valley, 1900–2000

historic core. Much of this growth actually perpetuates development directions that were established as early as the 1920s. In the vicinity of Fresno, Visalia and Porterville are subsidiary centers. At the southern end of the Valley, Bakersfield has also grown rapidly, especially toward the west, but also eastward toward higher elevations. Elsewhere, throughout the Valley, numerous small centers show evidence of growth, but none has matched the historic centers of growth.

Distribution and Density of Population

The San Joaquin Valley's urbanization pattern can be depicted statistically as well as geographically. Table 3.1 shows the population, urbanized acreage, and population density of the eight San Joaquin Valley counties in 2000, as well as totals for the three north Valley counties and the five south Valley counties.

Population density is typically measured as number of persons per urbanized acre of land. It provides a general idea of how densely populated an area is, but it does not depict the nature and character of development.

In general, California's urban population densities are far higher than the national average, even in the San Joaquin Valley. A 2001 study by the Brookings Institution Center on Urban and Metropolitan Policy—which used a different data source for urbanized land than this study did—found that urban population density nationwide was approximately 3.55 persons per urbanized acre (2,270 persons per square

Table 3.1

**Population, Urbanization, and Population Density in the
San Joaquin Valley, 2000**

County	Population	Urbanized Acres	Population Density[a]
North Valley	1,221,149	199,068	6.1
Merced	210,554	40,105	5.3
San Joaquin	563,598	86,126	6.5
Stanislaus	446,997	72,837	6.1
South Valley	2,081,643	390,167	5.3
Fresno	799,407	119,505	6.7
Kern	661,645	140,314	4.7
Kings	129,461	35,865	3.6
Madera	123,109	33,621	3.7
Tulare	368,021	60,862	6.0
Entire Valley	3,302,792	589,235	5.6

SOURCE: U.S. Census, 2000.

[a]Persons per acre of urbanized land.

mile) in 1997. The figure for California was double the national average, somewhere in the vicinity of seven persons per acre (4,480 per square mile).[1]

Using data from the state's Farmland Mapping and Monitoring Program (FMMP)[2] and the U.S. Census Bureau, in Table 3.1 we have calculated the number of urbanized acres and the population density for the eight counties in the San Joaquin Valley. The current population density of the San Joaquin Valley is 5.6 persons per urbanized acre (3,580 per square mile)—a figure that is significantly higher than the national average but substantially lower than the statewide average. Furthermore, there is considerable variation within the Valley. Some counties have a population density of close to seven persons per urbanized acre; others are well below four persons per acre.

In general, the "Bay spillover" counties in the north Valley have higher densities than the agricultural counties in the south Valley. However, two south Valley agricultural counties—Fresno and Tulare— had among the highest urban population densities in the San Joaquin Valley. This is not necessarily the result of more compact development patterns in these counties, although local planning policies may well account for part of the density. It could also be a function of household size.

Population density statistics are different from measurements of building density. That is, they do not seek to measure units per acre, as do typical planning and zoning ordinances. Rather, they measure the number of people occupying one acre of urbanized space. In that sense, this statistic is sensitive not only to compact development but also to large households. Some parts of the San Joaquin Valley have large households and therefore the population density will be high. As we will see below, these tendencies may be in conflict with the urban development results of our model.

---

[1] Fulton et al. (2001).

[2] The FMMP falls within the California State Department of Conservation, Division of Land Resource Protection.

Existing Farmland

Because of its significance as the major land use, farmland deserves more detailed consideration. As of 2000, the eight counties of the San Joaquin Valley had about 5.7 million acres of farmland (see Table 3.2). Of this, about 3.2 million, or 55.6 percent, was classified by the state as prime farmland—that is, land that has the best combination of soil quality, growing season, and water supply, and actually was in irrigated agricultural production within four years of the mapping date.[3]

Another 1.4 million, or 24 percent, was defined as farmland of state importance even though it was not categorized as prime. Other categories of farmland made up the remaining 20 percent of the farmland in the eight counties.

As Figure 3.3 shows, the prime farmland is in a large northwest-to-southeast section of the San Joaquin Valley floor, stretching from the tip of San Joaquin County all the way south to Bakersfield. The Tulare Basin, which is largely in Kings County, consists mainly of farmland of statewide importance, although it is not categorized as prime farmland. Much of the farmland along the Highway 99 corridor is a mixture of these two categories, and some has been fragmented over time by urbanization.

Table 3.2

Type of Farmland in the San Joaquin Valley, 2000

Type of Farmland	Acres	% of Total
Prime farmland	3,187,349	55.6
Farmland of state importance	1,376,158	24.0
Farmland of unique significance	534,319	9.3
Farmland of local importance	116,936	2.0
Grazing	78,204	1.4
Other farmland	439,476	7.7
Total farmland	5,732,442	100.0

SOURCE: PPIC calculations, based on FMMP data.

---

[3]For detailed definitions of these categories see http://www.consrv.ca.gov/DLRP/fmmp/

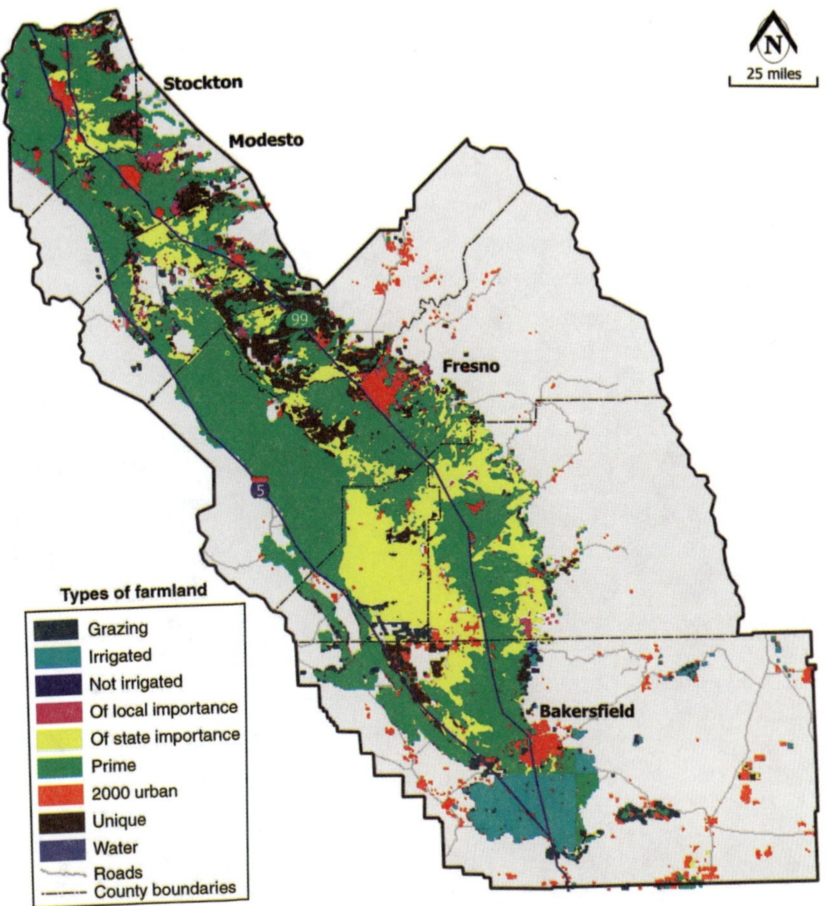

Figure 3.3—Type of Farmland in the San Joaquin Valley, 2000

Conclusion

In its land-use distribution at the beginning of the 21st century, the San Joaquin Valley remains a largely agricultural area with a growing but still limited degree of urbanization at moderate densities by U.S. standards. We now turn to the issue of future urban growth and how it may play out under alternative scenarios.

4. Urbanization Scenarios for the San Joaquin Valley

Over the next 40 years, the population of the San Joaquin Valley is expected to double to about seven million people—about the same population as the San Francisco Bay Area today. As with all estimates of future population, that figure is uncertain, but it reflects the middle of the range of alternative estimates available. The future character of the Valley will depend in large part on how that population is distributed across the landscape. The Valley is a vast canvas compared to California's coastal metropolitan areas—more than 20,000 square miles of land on the Valley floor, with few topographical barriers or blocks of public land ownership in place to shape the pattern of urbanization.

That urbanization could take many different forms. It could consist mostly of the low-density development that characterizes most new urban growth in the United States. It could look much like development in coastal California, with relatively high densities constructed in a low-rise, automobile-oriented pattern adjacent to existing communities. It could be concentrated along transportation routes in fairly high-density fashion. It could take some other form—or some combination of forms—that we cannot yet predict.

To provide some insight into what future urbanization patterns and their effect on the San Joaquin Valley might be, we created four possible future urbanization scenarios for the San Joaquin Valley. We used an urban growth model called SLEUTH, which stands for Slope, Landcover, Excluded, Urban extent, Transportation, Hillshade. It uses patterns and trends derived from historical data on urban growth to project the future shape and extent of urban areas.[1] This model was

---

[1] SLEUTH was developed by Professor Keith Clarke of the University of California, Santa Barbara (Clarke, Hoppen, and Gaydos, 1997). The appendix describes the model and its logic in more detail.

selected because it allows the construction of alternative futures without demanding an inordinate amount of research time and detailed data. Based on a geographic information system (GIS), the model not only generates dynamic maps of development over time but it also allows the creation of a wide variety of statistics that describe the urban pattern and its changes over time. The downside of this approach is that the scenarios will have a "broad brush" character. Without a great deal of information beyond what was available for this study, fine-grained forecasts with multiple land uses are difficult to construct.

Urban Development Scenarios

The four scenarios that were constructed for this study trace out and illustrate the consequences of varying constraints on future urban growth, assuming that underlying growth processes similar to those that have occurred in the past will continue to hold. In effect, the model reflects the patterns of past urban growth and can be used to project scenarios under various assumptions. The model uses information about the extent and speed of past urbanization in great geographic detail. It does not attempt to relate that information to specific factors such as population or employment that might be expected to drive growth. In this sense, it resembles a kind of trend analysis, but it incorporates the detailed spatial behavior of urbanization over time.

The four scenarios are as follows:

1. An *Accommodating Urban Development* scenario assumes that the underlying urbanization patterns of the last 60 years will continue 40 years into the future. This scenario assumes no significant regional constraints on urban growth beyond those implicit in the historic pattern of development, with its high level of infrastructure provision and few constraints on resources. Because the Valley has few natural obstacles such as mountains or water to impede growth, and because there is relatively little permanently protected land, such as that in national forests or state parks, this scenario will tend to give a maximum development outcome. This scenario makes no assumptions about specific transportation investments. Rather, it implicitly

assumes that accessibility levels will be adequate to permit development similar to that which has historically occurred.

2. A *Prime Farmland Conservation* scenario permits urbanization to continue following the historical pattern but prohibits urbanization of all 3.2 million acres of prime farmland in the San Joaquin Valley, as previously shown in Figure 3.3. Note that most of the land in the Tulare Basin and much land along Highway 99 is classified not as prime farmland but as farmland of statewide importance.[2] Thus, this land is available for urban development under this scenario. Politically and socially, it is unlikely that regulation of development at this scale could occur in the Valley, but as a scenario, it does reflect a concern for farmland preservation that is widely felt.

3. A *High-Speed Rail* scenario reflects proposals that are currently under consideration for a high-speed rail system that would connect the Bay Area and Sacramento to Los Angeles, via the San Joaquin Valley (Figure 4.1). Under this scenario, the model increases the probability of urbanization within a 20-mile radius of the stations tentatively identified as part of the proposed high-speed rail network, and decreases the relative probability of urbanization outside that 20-mile radius. Although there is no assurance that such a system will be built, it has been the focus of much interest in the San Joaquin Valley and provides a conceptual framework for a very different basic transportation structure.

4. An *Automobile-Oriented Managed Growth* scenario assumes that Highway 65, a north-south highway on the eastern side of the Valley, would be extended and upgraded to allow substantial capacity. In addition, several east-west routes would be improved, and the relative probability of new development would be increased along these transportation corridors and along Interstate 5 (Figure 4.2). Thus, this scenario sketches a future in which highway transportation improvements are made in the context of an effort to shape urban growth. It differs from

---

[2]These farmland categories are defined explicitly below.

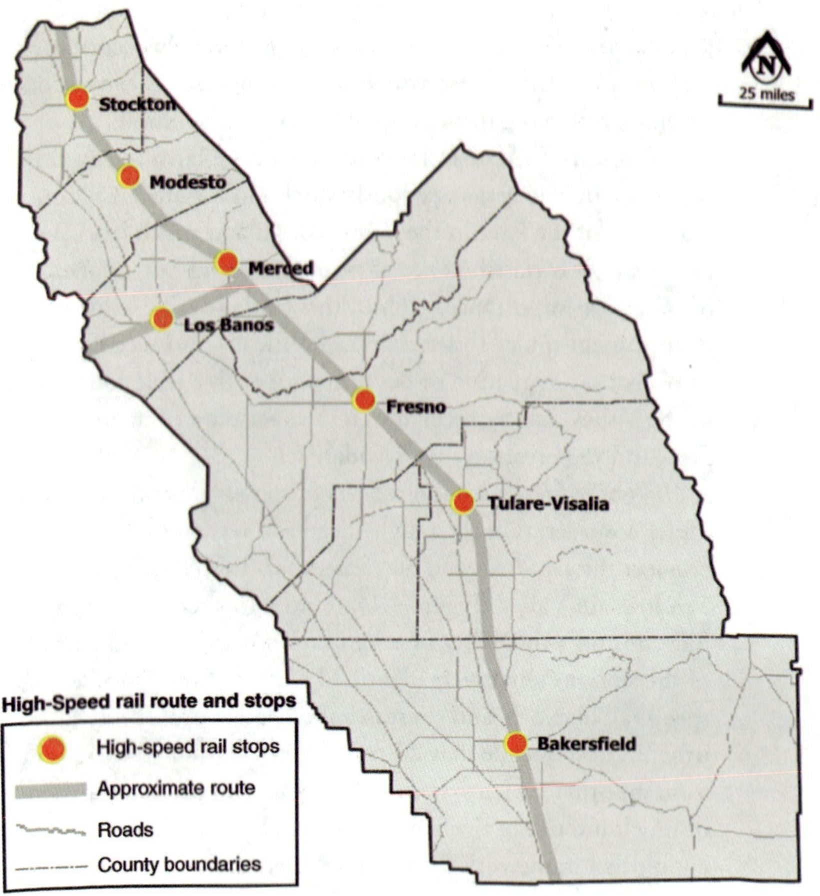

Figure 4.1—Proposed High-Speed Rail Route and Stops Assumed in the High-Speed Rail Scenario

the Accommodating Urban Development scenario in that it anticipates an automobile-oriented form of urbanization that also embodies a conscious attempt to influence future growth patterns.

The scenarios were developed over the course of the study with input from planners and decisionmakers. Clearly, they are not the only possible scenarios that could have been selected. However, in looking 40 years ahead, it is important to try to identify very broad factors affecting

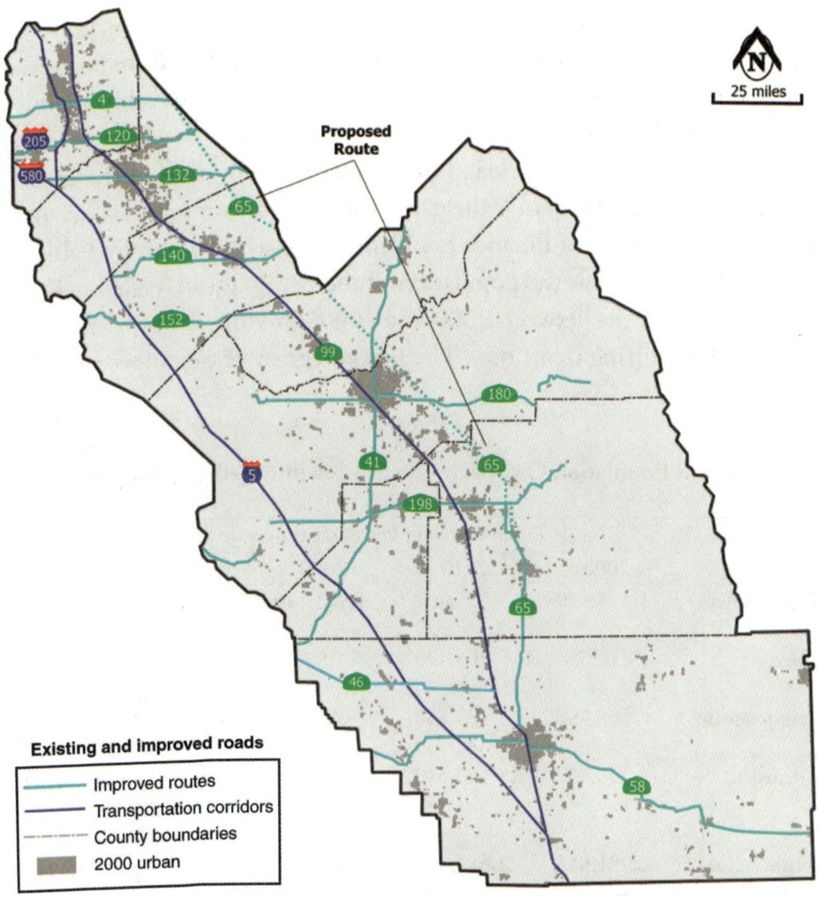

Figure 4.2—Improved Transportation Routes in the Automobile-Oriented Managed Growth Scenario

urban growth. A near-term change—for example, the development of the University of California at Merced—although it could be very important, would be unlikely to shape urbanization at the scale of the Valley any more than U.C. Riverside transformed the Inland Empire. It was necessary to construct a baseline case—the Accommodating Urban Development scenario—because that is the unconstrained output of the model. At the other extreme, restricting development on prime farmland provides an illustration of one of many possible scenarios focusing on agriculture. The two transportation-based scenarios provide insight into infrastructure policy, together with some implied management of growth. We would have liked to construct a scenario based on land-use policy, but the lack of Valley-wide data on land-use and development policies made that infeasible.

Each scenario was modeled at the county level for each of the eight counties in the San Joaquin Valley. To supplement our analysis, we use the state Department of Finance population forecasts, shown in Table 4.1, which suggest that the population of the San Joaquin Valley will increase 116 percent between 2000 and 2040, growing from 3.3 million to 7.3 million during that time. The percentage increase ranges from 90

Table 4.1

Projected Population Growth in the San Joaquin Valley, 2000–2040

County	Population and Percentage Increase from 2000				
	2000	2010	2020	2030	2040
North Valley	1,221,149	1,575,807	1,913,110	2,292,560	2,709,536
		29	57	88	122
Merced	210,554	264,420	319,785	385,120	460,020
		26	52	83	118
San Joaquin	563,598	725,868	884,375	1,060,442	1,250,610
		29	57	88	122
Stanislaus	446,997	585,519	708,950	846,998	998,906
		31	59	89	123
South Valley	2,081,643	2,612,533	3,169,225	3,833,975	4,594,399
		26	52	84	121
Fresno	799,407	953,457	1,114,403	1,308,767	1,521,360
		19	39	64	90
Kern	661,645	859,818	1,073,748	1,327,013	1,623,671
		30	62	101	145
Kings	129,461	154,617	186,611	223,914	265,944
		19	44	73	105
Madera	123,109	175,132	224,567	281,300	346,451
		42	82	128	181
Tulare	368,021	469,509	569,896	692,981	836,973
		28	55	88	127
Entire Valley	3,302,792	4,188,340	5,082,335	6,126,535	7,303,935
		27	54	85	121

SOURCE: California State Department of Finance.

percent in Fresno County to 181 percent in Madera County. It should be borne in mind, however, that population growth does not directly drive our urbanization model.

We analyzed each of the eight counties separately, estimating the growth in urban area over time in each.[3] SLEUTH does not explicitly incorporate population change, but insofar as any analysis of the implications for population is conducted, the population increase in each county remains the same in all scenarios, and different scenarios do not transfer population growth from one county to another. In addition, in all four scenarios, no urban development occurs on publicly owned land.

Limitations of SLEUTH

SLEUTH is a "cellular automata" urban growth model that seeks to predict the geographical pattern of future urban growth by dividing the area into "cells" and assigning a probability of future development of each cell using criteria provided to the model. Using SLEUTH requires the development and compilation of historical data (transportation networks, urbanization patterns, and other data) associated with urban growth and development.

The basic probability of a cell being urbanized is influenced by a series of assumptions about how growth occurs. These assumptions have proven generally valid in most settings. For example, urban growth tends to occur adjacent to existing urban areas, in new urban centers in close proximity to (but separated from) existing urban areas, and along transportation networks. The model is "calibrated"—that is, the use of these assumptions is adjusted—so that it can accurately recreate past growth patterns. More detail about SLEUTH, the datasets used in creating and calibrating it, and the assumptions behind the scenarios is contained in the appendix.

Although the model provides the ability to view the geographical pattern of future urban growth—and to measure the amount of land-use change in acres—it does not seek to depict or describe the quality or

---

[3]We also analyzed the Valley as a single unit. The results from aggregating individual estimates were judged to be more satisfactory.

character of that growth. Thus, it cannot distinguish between residential and nonresidential development. Likewise, its results suggest an increase or decrease in density based on the amount of land being urbanized, but it cannot depict or forecast patterns of specific subdivisions, the size and character of building lots, or the demographics and size of individual households.

In using this model for the San Joaquin Valley, we have defined "urban" land as FMMP defines it:

> Land occupied by structures with a building density of at least 1 unit to 1.5 acres, or approximately 6 structures to a 10-acre parcel. This land is used for residential, industrial, commercial, construction, institutional, public administration, railroad and other transportation yards, cemeteries, airports, golf courses, sanitary landfills, sewage treatment, water control structures, and other developed purposes (http://www.consrv.ca.gov/DLRP/fmmp/).

"Urbanization" refers to the transformation of any other land use type (field, forest, swamp, etc.) to one of those listed above.

It is important to note that these scenarios represent only conditional forecasts or predictions of the probable patterns of urban growth under the specific assumptions on which they are developed. They do not incorporate specific predictions of how other policy scenarios or public investments would influence the pattern of growth. Nor do they take explicit account of such factors as zoning, local growth control, or other public policy. Indeed, the assumptions in all these scenarios are unrealistic to some degree. It is unlikely, for example, that any state and local farmland preservation policy would result in the preservation of all prime farmland in the Central Valley, no matter where it is located. It is also unlikely that the construction of the high-speed rail system would drive most urban growth within a 20-mile radius of the stations, if only because urban development is driven by local as well as regional considerations.

Rather, it is best to view the four scenarios simply as four different ways to look at future possibilities. By examining these four diverse scenarios, it is possible to sense the range of forms that future urban growth will take and to examine the effect of that future urban growth. They should be viewed as a starting point for a conversation about how future urban growth might affect the Valley, and what public policy interventions might be worth pursuing as a means of altering the growth pattern for the better.

5. Future Valleys: Results of the Four Growth Scenarios

No matter what the San Joaquin Valley's future population growth path may be, the effect of that growth could vary dramatically depending on the urbanization pattern that emerges. This chapter first provides an overview, comparing the four scenarios, then discusses specifically how each scenario would affect urbanization patterns and the loss of farmland.

Overview of the Scenarios

One overriding question is how much land will urban growth consume? Table 5.1 suggests that urbanized land would increase significantly by 2040 under all scenarios. The Accommodating Urban Development scenario increases urbanized land by 322 percent, to 2.5 million acres. Under the Prime Farmland Conservation scenario, urbanized land would increase by 134 percent, to almost 1.4 million acres. The two transportation-related scenarios imply a tripling of urbanized land, to between 1.7 million and 1.9 million acres.

Gross population densities would also be very different under each scenario. If the San Joaquin Valley were to have the predicted population of 7.3 million in 2040, then the Accommodating Urban Development scenario would imply a 47 percent drop to about 3.1 persons per urbanized acre, or fewer than 2,000 persons per square mile. The Prime Farmland Conservation scenario would result in a density of 5.5 persons per acre, a drop of only about 4.6 percent. The Automobile-Oriented Managed Growth scenario leads to a 21.6 percent decline, to 4.8 persons per urbanized acre, and the High-Speed Rail scenario leads to a larger decline (33.2 percent), to 4.0 persons per acre.

These levels of density are sufficiently different from the present ones to raise questions about whether the estimates of urbanized area are too

Table 5.1

Changes in Urbanized Land Acreage in the San Joaquin Valley Under Four Scenarios, 2000–2040

	2000	Accommodating Urban Development	Prime Farmland Conservation	High-Speed Rail	Automobile-Oriented Managed Growth
North Valley					
Total acreage	199,068	798,199	389,737	714,496	560,853
Increase 2000–2040		605,615	190,669	515,428	361,785
% increase		314	96	254	182
South Valley					
Total acreage	390,167	1,689,906	987,817	1,195,491	1,136,876
Increase 2000–2040		1,293,255	597,650	805,324	746,709
% increase		326	153	206	191
Entire Valley					
Total acreage	589,235	2,488,105	1,377,554	1,909,987	1,697,729
Increase 2000–2040		1,898,870	788,319	1,320,752	1,108,494
% increase		322	134	224	188

SOURCE: Authors' estimates.

high or the population projections too low. Population estimates vary, but those we have used fall close to the middle of projections by different researchers. There are few other estimates of urbanization with which to compare those developed here. Landis and Reilly (2003) estimated significantly lower levels of urbanization in the Valley for 2050, but their initial measure of urbanization in 1998 is much lower than the estimate used in this study.[1] Their corresponding estimate of gross urban population density actually shows a significant increase. This uncertainty should reinforce the view that the scenarios are best viewed as providing comparative insight about alternative futures rather than precise forecasts of any specific future.

---

[1] It is not immediately evident why this should be the case, but it may be related to differences in the definition of urbanized land and the base year estimates used.

The differences in farmland loss between the scenarios are also significant, as shown in Table 5.2. Not surprisingly, the Accommodating Urban Development scenario results in the largest farmland loss—1.5 million acres of farmland (26 percent of the total) and 924,000 acres of prime farmland (29 percent of the total). By definition, the Prime Farmland Conservation scenario results in no loss of prime farmland; nevertheless, some 445,000 acres of other farmland is lost, resulting in an overall drop of close to 8 percent. Again, the two transportation-oriented scenarios wind up in the middle, with farmland loss of between 14 percent and 20 percent. In the three scenarios where prime farmland is lost, about 60 percent of that total consists of prime farmland and 40 percent is made up of other farmland.

It should be emphasized again that the urbanization model provides no direct evidence of the nature or quality of the urban development required to accommodate this growth. However, the differences in these scenarios' results suggest that the character of development will be

Table 5.2

Loss of Farmland Acreage in the San Joaquin Valley Under Four Scenarios, 2000–2040

	Current	Accommodating Urban Development	Prime Farmland Conservation	High-Speed Rail	Automobile-Oriented Managed Growth
Prime farmland					
Total acreage	3,187,349	2,262,970	3,187,349	2,521,332	2,680,188
Acreage loss		924,379	—	666,017	507,161
% loss		29	—	20.9	15.9
Other farmland					
Total acreage	2,545,093	1,955,546	2,099,587	2,120,749	2,219,039
Acreage loss		589,547	445,505	427,613	329,323
% loss		23.2	17.5	16.8	12.9
Total farmland					
Total acreage	5,732,442	4,218,516	5,286,936	4,642,081	4,899,227
Acreage loss		1,513,926	445,505	1,093,630	836,484
% loss		26.4	7.8	19.1	14.6

SOURCE: Authors' estimates.

significantly different and will have a profound effect on the Valley's landscape. The specific scenarios that follow provide some indication of what that effect might be.

Accommodating Urban Development

This scenario projects the Valley's urban growth from its historical pattern. The result is a dramatic pattern of scattered urban development up and down the Valley, especially along Highway 99 (Figure 5.1). Most new development would be near existing communities, with a

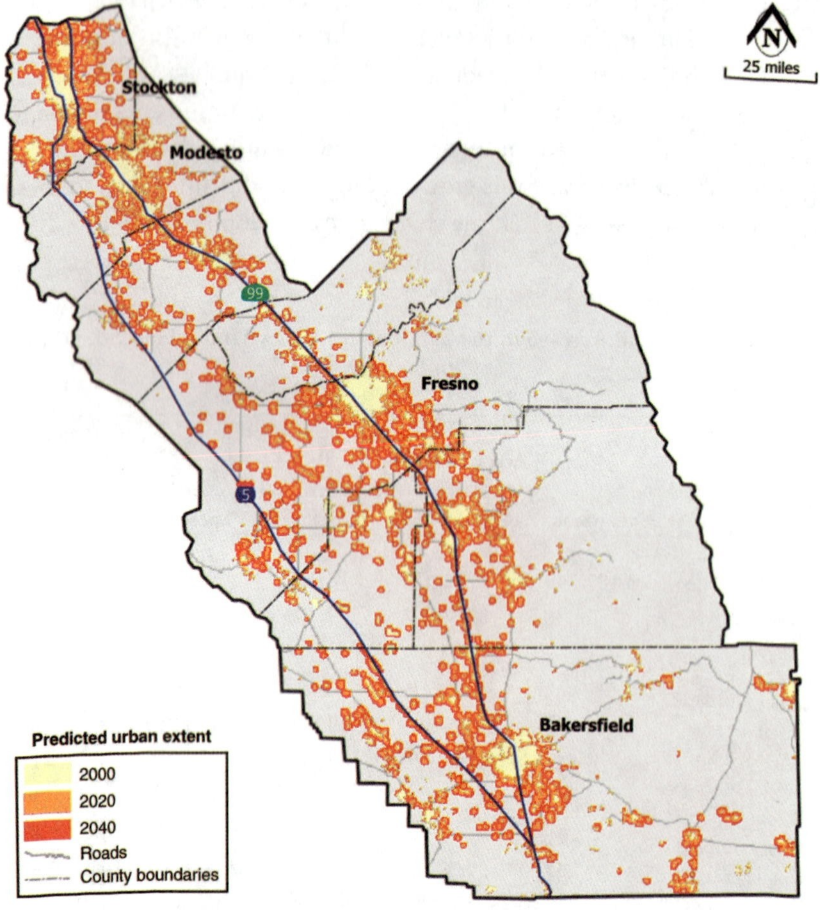

Figure 5.1—Geographical Pattern of Urbanization Under the Accommodating Urban Development Scenario, 2000–2040

notable coalescing of cities in the counties adjacent to the Bay Area. It is likely that the development would have a low-density, sprawling character, especially in the agricultural counties in the south Valley, Valley-wide, urbanized land would increase by 422 percent, from 589,000 acres to almost 2.5 million acres (Table 5.3). This increase would be somewhat greater in the south Valley than in the north Valley. In absolute terms, Fresno and Kern Counties would see the greatest increase in urbanized area (about 500,000 acres each). In percentage terms, Merced and Tulare Counties would increase the most (about 400 percent), whereas Madera and Stanislaus Counties would increase the least (134 percent and 203 percent, respectively).

If population were to grow as forecast, the imputed population densities would decline significantly throughout the Valley. Fresno County would decrease its gross urban density by 60 percent, from 6.8 to 2.8 persons per acre. As a matter of comparison, 6.8 persons per acre is typical of the tightly packed, automobile-oriented development patterns typically seen in suburban California in the last 20 years. However, 2.8 persons per acre would be closer to the sprawling suburban

Table 5.3

Urbanized Acreage in the San Joaquin Valley Under the Accommodating Urban Development Scenario, by County, 2000–2040

County	2000	2040	Change	% Change
North Valley	199,068	798,199	599,131	301
Merced	40,105	208,001	167,896	419
San Joaquin	86,126	369,488	283,362	329
Stanislaus	72,837	220,711	147,874	203
South Valley	390,167	1,689,906	1,299,739	333
Fresno	119,505	545,158	425,653	356
Kern	140,314	644,063	503,749	359
Kings	35,865	124,310	88,445	247
Madera	33,621	78,697	45,076	134
Tulare	60,862	297,678	236,816	389
Entire Valley	589,235	2,488,106	1,898,870	322

SOURCE: Authors' estimates.

NOTE: Acreage amounts may not sum to totals because of rounding.

development patterns of the Midwest and South, where most new houses sit on quarter- and half-acre lots.

Most other counties would see similar declines in density, suggesting that the predominant development pattern would consist of large-lot subdivisions that are often not contiguous with current urban development and very low-density exurban development. This pattern could place both farmland and habitat at greater risk than would be the case under other scenarios.

Even in the north Valley, where development has historically been more dense, significant declines in density would occur, especially in Merced and San Joaquin Counties. Indeed, San Joaquin County—the county receiving perhaps the most Bay Area urbanization pressure— would see almost a 50 percent drop in density, from 6.7 persons per urbanized acre to 3.4 persons per urbanized acre. In this scenario as in all the others, Madera County is the outlier, showing a slight increase in population density.[2]

The Accommodating Urban Development scenario would also result in a significant loss of both prime and nonprime farmland (Table 5.4).

Table 5.4

Farmland Acreage Loss in the San Joaquin Valley Under the Accommodating Urban Development Scenario, 2000–2040

Type of Farmland	Current	Accommodating Urban Development	Loss	% Loss
Prime farmland	3,187,349	2,262,970	924,379	29.0
Farmland of statewide importance	1,376,158	1,071,826	304,332	22.1
Unique farmland	534,319	440,736	93,583	17.5
Farmland of local importance	116,936	72,696	44,240	37.8
Grazing land	78,204	63,180	15,024	19.2
Other farmland	439,476	307,108	132,368	30.2
Total	5,732,442	4,218,516	1,513,926	26.4

SOURCE: Authors' estimates.

---

[2]In much of this analysis, the pattern for Madera County differs from that of other counties. That may be attributable to the way the model is calibrated. It was not possible to fully account for these results.

It would result in an overall loss of 1.5 million acres of agricultural land—a 26.4 percent decline—including almost one million acres of prime farmland.[3] Much of the prime farmland lost is around the urban fringes of many of the major cities in San Joaquin Valley. Because farming communities were created in prime farmland areas—along what is now the Highway 99 corridor—the urbanization of land immediately adjacent to these population centers results in a major farmland loss. Farmlands of state importance and projected to urbanize in this scenario are interspersed among the peripheral prime farmland.[4] A majority of the grazing land that is expected to be lost to urbanization by 2040 under this scenario is along the eastern and western boundaries of the San Joaquin Valley and in its southernmost portion.

In sum, the Accommodating Urban Development scenario projects huge urban growth at very low densities. It would truly transform the Valley as we now know it. However, the scenario should not be interpreted literally. It represents only one conceivable future for the Valley—most likely one at the far end of the spectrum. At the other end of the spectrum is a much more restrictive growth scenario, which will be considered next.

Prime Farmland Conservation

This scenario examines how urbanization would occur if prime farmland were protected but development otherwise occurred according to historical patterns. The model prohibits development on the 3.2 million acres in the San Joaquin Valley characterized as prime farmland by the state FMMP.

This scenario creates less urbanized land than any other scenario. Because prime farmland is concentrated around the existing Valley communities along Highway 99, most of the land adjacent to these communities—slated for development in most other scenarios—remains in farmland under this scenario. But as Figure 5.2 shows, it would not

---

[3]Recall that the definitions of farmland used here are those from the FMMP. What FMMP considered "prime" might be different from other agencies' definitions.

[4]Farmlands of state importance constitute a category within the FMMP classification.

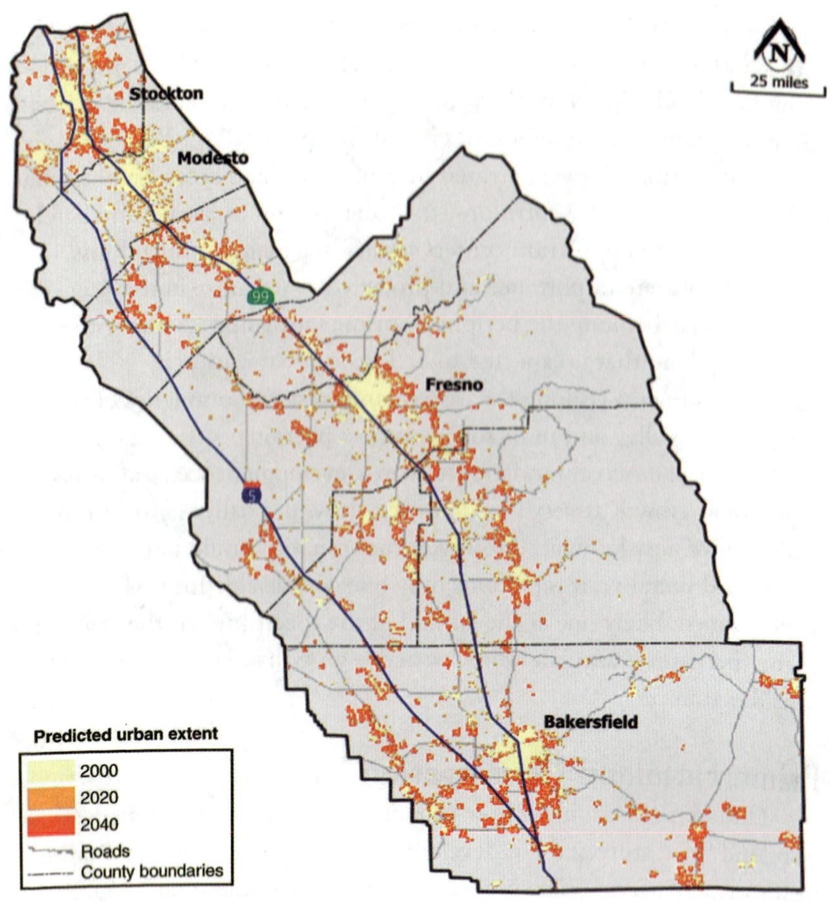

Figure 5.2—Geographical Pattern of Urbanization Under the Prime Farmland
Conservation Scenario, 2000–2040

necessarily result in a contiguous development pattern. Urbanized areas
do not aggregate near existing towns or even near each other. This is
because nonprime farmland follows no particular pattern that is related
to previous urbanization. For example, little additional urbanization
occurs along the Highway 99 corridor because existing towns straddle
some of the best farmland, which would be protected under this
scenario.

At the same time, much scattered development would occur on the
west side of the Valley, especially in Kings and Kern Counties, because

these areas contain many pockets of nonprime farmland. These lands may or may not be next to roads or to the other infrastructure required to accommodate urban growth. Thus, this scenario scatters development across the Valley to save prime farmland.

Despite its restrictions, the Prime Farmland Conservation scenario still increases urbanization from 589,000 acres to 1.37 million acres; but the increase of 134 percent is far less than in any other scenario (Table 5.5). Urban conversion is much less prevalent in the north Valley than in the south Valley, largely because it would permit only a 4 percent increase in urbanization in Stanislaus County, from 72,800 to 75,400 acres. Urbanization around Fresno would also not be nearly as great as in other scenarios. Kern County—home to relatively little prime farmland—would experience the most urbanization in both raw numbers and percentage terms. Merced, Kings, and Tulare Counties would also see relatively large increases in urbanization.

Several major metropolitan areas are prevented from growing, except in certain directions. In all of the other scenarios, there was a coalescing of urban areas between Stockton and Modesto. By precluding growth

Table 5.5

Urbanized Acreage in the San Joaquin Valley Under the Prime Farmland Conservation Scenario, by County, 2000–2040

County	2000	2040	Change	% Change
North Valley	199,068	389,737	190,669	96
Merced	40,105	119,155	79,050	197
San Joaquin	86,126	195,175	109,049	127
Stanislaus	72,837	75,408	2,571	4
South Valley	390,167	987,817	597,650	153
Fresno	119,505	220,582	101,076	85
Kern	140,314	445,924	305,611	218
Kings	35,865	96,101	60,236	168
Madera	33,621	65,354	31,733	94
Tulare	60,862	159,856	98,994	163
Entire Valley	589,235	1,377,554	788,319	134

SOURCE: Authors' estimates.

NOTE: Acreage amounts may not sum to totals because of rounding.

on prime farmland, however, this scenario prevents cities from merging together into one large urban area. Other cities, including Fresno, Bakersfield, and Tulare-Visalia, exhibit similar trends, where urbanization is precluded from moving in one or more directions.

Overall, imputed population density declines slightly, from 5.72 persons per urbanized acre to 5.46—the smallest decline of any scenario. There is a significant difference between the north Valley (which would experience a 10 percent increase, to 7.0 persons per acre) and the south Valley (which would experience a 10 percent decrease, to 4.9 persons per acre).

As stated above, the increase in the north Valley density is due almost entirely to Stanislaus County, where virtually all the remaining undeveloped land is prime farmland. To accommodate the expected population growth, Stanislaus County's population density would double to more than 13 persons per acre. This population density, which is similar to that of Los Angeles, is not plausible on its face.

The Prime Farmland Conservation scenario also causes densities to hold at high levels—between 6.7 and 7 persons per acre—in the south Valley counties with the richest agricultural land, specifically Madera, Fresno, and Tulare Counties. Rather than trending toward less density, as would be the case if historic patterns were continued, these counties continue to accommodate new population at about the same density as the current average. Not surprisingly, Kern and Kings Counties—which have less prime farmland and would, as noted above, experience considerable scattered urban development under this scenario—would see a drop in population density of about 21 percent.

As Table 5.6 shows, there would still be farmland loss of about 445,000 acres—almost 9 percent—even under the Prime Farmland Conservation scenario. This is largely because development that would otherwise occur on prime farmland would be shifted to other agricultural lands, most notably farmland of statewide importance, which would account for more than half the loss. This is another reason why Kings and Kern Counties would receive scattered urban development. Much agricultural land of statewide importance is in these counties, principally because of the presence of the Tulare Basin.

Table 5.6

Farmland Acreage Loss in the San Joaquin Valley Under the Prime
Farmland Conservation Scenario

Type of Farmland	Current	Prime Farmland Conservation	Loss	% Loss
Prime farmland	3,187,349	3,187,349	—	—
Farmland of statewide importance	1,376,158	1,146,958	229,199	16.7
Unique farmland	534,319	472,666	61,653	11.5
Farmland of local importance	116,936	87,405	29,531	25.3
Grazing land	78,204	65,562	12,641	16.2
Other farmland	439,476	326,996	112,481	
Total	5,732,441	5,286,936	445,505	7.8

SOURCE: Authors' estimates.

NOTE: Acreage amounts may not sum to totals because of rounding.

In sum, the Prime Farmland Conservation scenario presents an unrealistic picture but nonetheless provides food for thought. It brings out the extent to which future growth in the Valley would impinge on the prime farmland resource. Conversely, it presents the question of how agriculture is to continue as a major source of economic activity and income in the coming decades if urban growth is extensive. It may well be that the farm sector can shift to land of lesser quality, but the full costs and benefits of that transition need to be considered.

High-Speed Rail

This scenario is predicated on the possibility that a new rail transportation system will be constructed through the Valley, with stations to be built at locations envisioned by the California High-Speed Rail Authority. It further assumes that the construction of this system will significantly influence development patterns in the Valley. More specifically, it is structured on the simplifying assumption that development is much more likely within a 20-mile radius of the stations and much less likely outside that 20-mile radius.

As currently proposed, the rail route would have seven stops within the San Joaquin Valley. These would be in Stockton (San Joaquin County), Modesto (Stanislaus County), Los Banos (Merced County), Merced (Merced County), Fresno (Fresno County), Tulare-Visalia

(Tulare County), and Bakersfield (Kern County). As Figure 5.3 reveals, the resulting pattern creates by far the most focused development pattern of any of the four scenarios, with development highly concentrated around existing communities along the Highway 99 corridor. This reflects the fact that virtually all the high-speed rail stations would be in the existing large communities along Highway 99.

The High-Speed Rail scenario results in less urbanization than in the Accommodating Urban Development scenario but more than in the

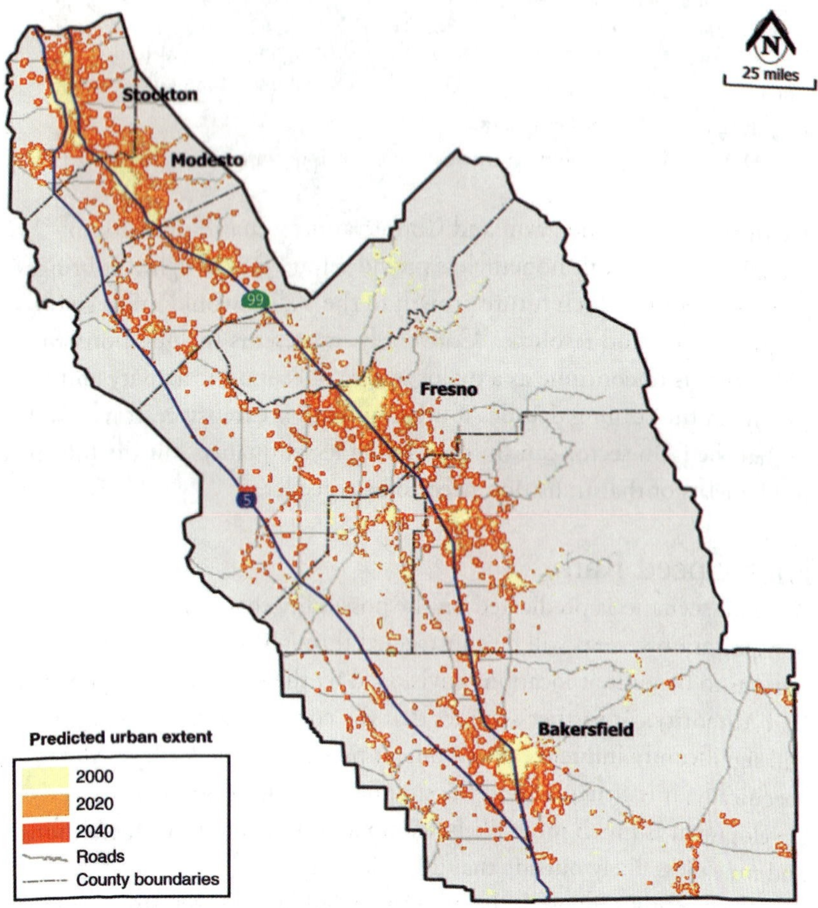

Figure 5.3—Geographical Pattern of Urbanization Under the High-Speed Rail Scenario, 2000–2040

Prime Farmland Conservation scenario. Whereas the latter scenario
would result in about 1.3 million urbanized acres, the High-Speed Rail
scenario would result in about 1.9 million urbanized acres—an increase
of 224 percent, or about midway between the two previous scenarios (see
Table 5.7). This scenario also leads to a different distribution of
urbanization within the Valley. Whereas the previous two scenarios
would lead to a greater percentage increase in urbanization in the south
Valley, the High-Speed Rail scenario would cause greater urbanization in
the north Valley. Four of the seven stations would be in three north
Valley counties. In practice, it might well be that some of this
development would be offset by new growth in Kern County spilling
over from Los Angeles. Our model cannot take account of that
possibility at this point.

Urbanization levels in San Joaquin and Stanislaus Counties are
almost as high as in the Accommodating Urban Development scenario.
Urbanization levels in Fresno and Kern Counties are much lower than in
the other scenarios.

Table 5.7

Urbanized Acreage in the San Joaquin Valley Under the High-Speed Rail Scenario, by County, 2000–2040

County	2000	2040	Change	% Change
North Valley	199,068	714,496	515,428	259
Merced	40,105	184,745	144,640	361
San Joaquin	86,126	322,409	236,283	274
Stanislaus	72,837	207,343	134,506	185
South Valley	390,167	1,195,491	805,324	206
Fresno	119,505	384,894	265,389	222
Kern	140,314	438,569	298,255	213
Kings	35,865	77,115	41,250	115
Madera	33,621	56,863	23,242	69
Tulare	60,862	238,051	177,189	291
Entire Valley	589,235	1,909,988	1,320,753	224

SOURCE: Authors' estimates.

NOTE: Acreage amounts may not sum to totals because of rounding.

Surprisingly, imputed population densities are still relatively low under the High-Speed Rail scenario—more than under any scenario except for Accommodating Urban Development. Densities drop significantly everywhere except Madera and Kings Counties, which have no rail stop. Even in the three North Valley counties, where most rail stops would be constructed, densities would drop significantly.

Although this outcome may seem counterintuitive at first, it is most likely a function of the development probabilities assumed in the High-Speed Rail scenario. Again, the model does not speak to the quality or character of urban development—only to the extent of urbanization. The key assumption in this scenario—that development would be more likely within 20 miles of a high-speed rail station—leads to concentrated growth near the existing population centers along Highway 99. But it does not force growth to be so compact that densities are increased. In other words, higher densities would require tighter regulation.

Without subcounty analysis, it is hard to characterize the likely character of the development pattern associated with the High-Speed Rail scenario. Certainly, most development would occur adjacent to existing communities along Highway 99, and the pattern would be more concentrated than would be the case under either the Accommodating Urban Development or the Prime Farmland Conservation scenarios. However, the overall densities do drop considerably from current levels. This decline suggests that even though development would be more concentrated around current population centers, it would most likely be automobile-oriented and would possibly involve larger lots than has historically been the case. However, none of this takes into account the possibility of local development control efforts, either to increase or to decrease the density of development within the range of rail stations.

Although the High-Speed Rail scenario creates a more concentrated development pattern, it still leads to a sizeable amount of farmland loss. As Table 5.8 shows, this scenario would lead to a loss of about one million acres of farmland (19% of the total), including some 666,000 acres of prime farmland (21%). These large losses result because the high-speed rail line would run along the Highway 99 corridor, the location of some of the richest farmland in the state. If the rail line

Table 5.8

Farmland Acreage Loss in the San Joaquin Valley Under the High-Speed
Rail Scenario, 2000–2040

Type of Farmland	Current	High-Speed Rail	Loss	% Loss
Prime farmland	3,187,349	2,521,332	666,017	20.9
Farmland of statewide importance	1,376,158	1,162,345	213,813	15.5
Unique farmland	534,319	466,182	68,137	12.8
Farmland of local importance	116,936	79,820	37,116	31.7
Grazing land	78,204	69,412	8,792	11.2
Other farmland	439,476	339,820	99,656	22.7
Total	5,732,441	4,638,910	1,093,531	19.1

SOURCE: Authors' estimates.

NOTE: Acreage amounts may not sum to totals because of rounding.

draws development toward existing population centers along Highway 99, it may cause a significant loss of farmland.

To summarize, our model suggests that a High-Speed Rail system would concentrate urban development but that the extent of growth would depend heavily on the accompanying regulatory structure. Such a system could provide a way of structuring urbanization in ways rarely seen in the United States but more common in Europe.

Automobile-Oriented Managed Growth

The final scenario, Automobile-Oriented Managed Growth, assumes a set of major highway improvements throughout the San Joaquin Valley as a way to facilitate and shape urbanization. Such a scenario builds explicitly on the existing dominant pattern of the Valley, which is automobile driven, but it would also include some constraints on the location of growth. Specifically, it assumes upgrades to most major east-west routes across the Valley (beginning with Route 4 in the north and proceeding all the way to Route 58 in the south), as well as the construction of significant portions of Highway 65, a north-south route along the east side of the Valley near the foothills. The model then raises the probability of urbanization near these transportation improvements, while reducing the probability of urbanization farther away from them, in effect mimicking growth management in a very broad sense.

The resulting urbanization pattern concentrates development along these transportation improvements—most particularly along the east-west routes in the north Valley (Routes 4, 120, and 132) and along Highway 65 on the east side of the Valley farther south (Figure 5.4). Partly because of the predominance of east-west routes especially in the north Valley, this scenario creates linear cities in some areas where urban

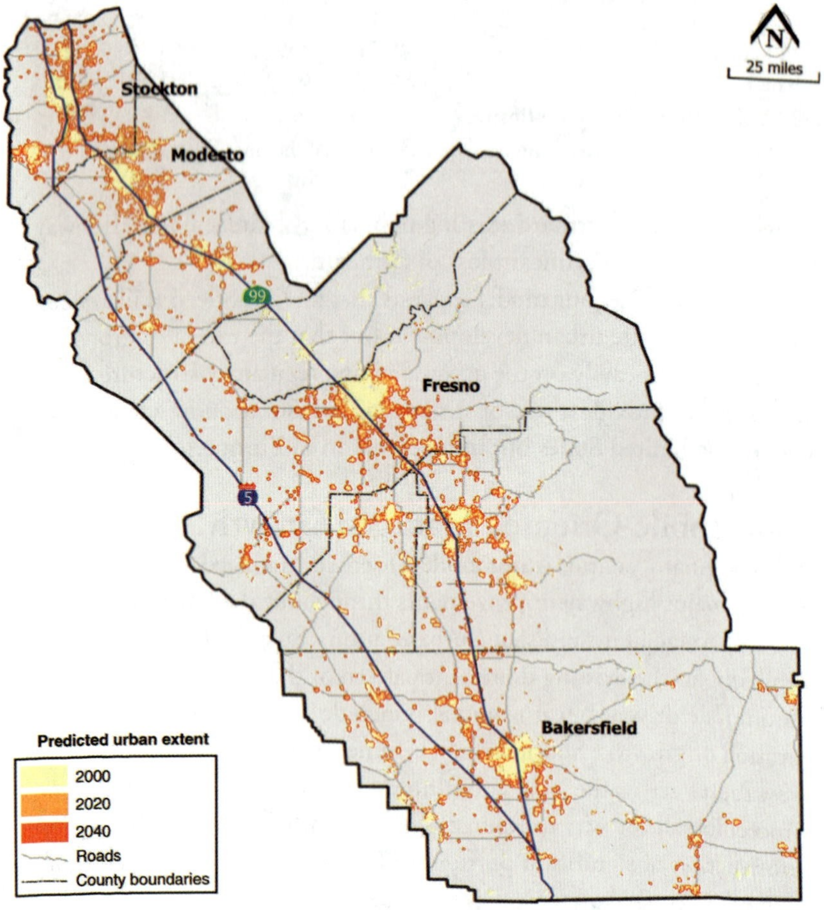

Figure 5.4—Geographical Pattern of Urbanization Under the Automobile-Oriented Managed Growth Scenario, 2000–2040

growth connected previously unconnected areas. This pattern is especially apparent in San Joaquin County, where urban growth connects Stockton with Tracy, Lodi, Manteca, Ripon, and Escalon. It affects Fresno, which begins to exhibit a radial pattern of growth with "spokes" extending from an urban core, as well the development of a Tulare-Visalia-Hanford-Lemoore urban corridor.

Surprisingly, overall urbanization is actually slightly less in this scenario than in the high-speed rail scenario—increasing 188 percent to about 1.7 million acres (Table 5.9). Like the High-Speed Rail scenario results, this is more or less a midpoint between the Accommodating Urban Development and the Prime Farmland Conservation scenarios. In percentage terms, development is fairly evenly distributed up and down the Valley. The largest percentage increase is experienced in Tulare County, where many of the Highway 65 improvements would be constructed. Neither Kings nor Madera Counties would experience significant increases in urban growth, largely because the scenario saw no improved transportation routes within their boundaries.

Table 5.9

Urbanized Acreage in the San Joaquin Valley Under the Automobile-Oriented Managed Growth Scenario, by County, 2000–2040

County	2000	2040	Change	% Change
North Valley	199,068	560,853	361,785	182
Merced	40,105	138,356	98,251	245
San Joaquin	86,126	259,916	173,790	202
Stanislaus	72,837	162,581	89,744	123
South Valley	390,167	1,136,876	746,709	191
Fresno	119,505	356,435	236,930	198
Kern	140,314	394,935	254,621	181
Kings	35,865	84,066	48,201	134
Madera	33,621	41,524	7,903	24
Tulare	60,862	259,916	199,054	327
Entire Valley	589,235	1,697,729	1,108,493	188

SOURCE: Authors' estimates.

NOTE: Acreage amounts may not sum to totals because of rounding.

The Automobile-Oriented Managed Growth scenario also leads to higher imputed urban densities than does the High-Speed Rail scenario—4.49 persons per urbanized acre Valley-wide compared to 3.82. This appears to result because growth clusters around the improved transportation corridors and is not as concentrated around existing urban areas. These declines are fairly consistent in both the north Valley and the south Valley.

With the exception of Madera County, which again is unlike the others, the county that holds its imputed population density closest to current levels is Stanislaus, where densities would remain unchanged at 6.1 persons per urbanized acre. (The other north Valley counties show much larger drops.) This is probably because the Automobile-Oriented Managed Growth scenario envisions significant east-west highway improvements through Stanislaus County, thus causing development to aggregate close to those corridors. In the south Valley, Kings and Kern Counties also show only a small decline in density, perhaps because of east-west improvements and (in Kern's case) the assumed construction of portions of Highway 65.

As with the High-Speed Rail scenario, it is difficult to assess the character of development and its effect on the Valley's overall landscape with this scenario. Although the overall population density would be higher than in the High-Speed Rail scenario, the resulting development pattern would be somewhat patchier. New growth would be scattered along highway corridors, and it would be less dense than the historical average. This too suggests that development would probably be of traditional suburban character. However, the Automobile-Oriented Managed Growth scenario would disrupt the Valley's present landscape less dramatically than either the Accommodating Urban Development or the Prime Farmland Conservation scenarios because of this concentration along highways. Motorists might well think that the Valley had been excessively urbanized because they would see more urban areas along the highways, but in rural areas, most of the Valley's landscape would be protected. On the other hand, this pattern might also encourage very low-density development on large parcels, if that were permitted.

The Automobile-Oriented Managed Growth scenario would result in less farmland loss than the High-Speed Rail scenario—especially as regards prime farmland (Table 5.10). The scenario would yield a loss of 836,000 acres of farmland (14.6%), including 507,000 acres of prime farmland (15.9%). Other farmland categories, including farmland of local importance, suffer greater losses on a percentage basis. This is mainly because the Automobile-Oriented Managed Growth scenario distributes new growth along the east-west transportation corridors and along Highway 65, which are (in some cases) not as close to prime or state-significant farmland as is Highway 99.

In sum, this scenario provides a glimpse of what is probably the most likely urban future of the Valley under its regime of development and regulation. It preserves the automobile-oriented character of development with a moderate degree of growth management, albeit very grossly defined.

Table 5.10

Farmland Acreage Loss in the San Joaquin Valley Under the Automobile-Oriented Managed Growth Scenario, 2000–2040

Type of Farmland	Current	Automobile-Oriented Managed Growth	Loss	% Loss
Prime farmland	3,187,349	2,680,188	507,161	15.9
Farmland of statewide importance	1,376,158	1,205,206	170,951	12.4
Unique farmland	534,319	487,917	46,402	8.7
Farmland of local importance	116,936	89,068	27,868	23.8
Grazing land	78,204	70,440	7,764	9.9
Other farmland	439,476	363,249	76,227	17.3
Total	5,732,441	4,896,069	836,373	14.6

SOURCE: Authors' estimates.

NOTE: Acreage amounts may not sum to totals because of rounding.

Conclusion

It is best not to think of these scenarios literally as forecasts or predictions of what will occur. Indeed, two of them are more in the nature of extreme cases. Rather, they provide alternative pictures that can be used to compare outcomes and stimulate discussion about how the San Joaquin Valley might grow and what policy choices could be made to alter that growth pattern.

Bearing in mind the assumptions that underlie these scenarios, then, it is worth examining the differences and similarities between them.

There is little doubt that the San Joaquin Valley will continue to urbanize a large amount of land to accommodate population growth. Three of the four scenarios predicted urbanization of an additional one million acres of land or more—in essence, at least a tripling in the amount of urbanized land to accommodate a doubling of the population growth. This may seem unlikely, but it is not outside the experience of much of the United States in recent decades. Even with relatively dense housing development, other land uses, such as roads and highways, commercial and industrial development, warehousing and distribution, and public facilities, are prodigious users of land.

Second, the results suggest that the implied gross density of the urban population will decline. Again, three of the four scenarios imputed a major decline in densities over the next 40 years. This is not surprising given the nature of the San Joaquin Valley, which is a vast flat plain consisting mostly of privately owned land, in a region where land prices are lower than in the coastal metropolitan areas. In all likelihood, the future of the San Joaquin Valley will consist of automobile-oriented, low-rise development at lower-than-current densities. This has significant implications for traffic congestion, air quality, and other side effects that we have not considered in this report. At the same time, that pattern is subject to public policy, and there is certainly no agreement that it will occur.

Third, it seems that the amount of agricultural land in the San Joaquin Valley will continue to decline, perhaps dramatically. With the exception of the Prime Farmland Conservation scenario, which by definition protected all prime farmland from urbanization, all scenarios showed a decline in farmland of at least 15 percent. Even the Prime Farmland Conservation scenario showed a decline in farmland of almost 9 percent, indicating that if urbanization pressure is as great as our model suggests, it will be impossible to retain all farmland in the future.

Fourth—and perhaps most important—is that clear tradeoffs exist between the different scenarios, and that public policy could play a role in shaping the Valley's urban form depending on which policy goals are emphasized.

The Prime Farmland Conservation scenario moved a significant amount of development off prime farmland near current population centers along Highway 99, distributing it throughout the Valley to locations where prime farmland does not exist but where farmland of statewide significance does exist. By contrast, the High-Speed Rail scenario focuses development along the Highway 99 corridor—and although that development is more concentrated and less patchy than in any other scenario, it also consumes a large amount of prime farmland near the existing cities. Meanwhile, the Automobile-Oriented Managed Growth scenario scatters development along highway corridors, assuring that new development is auto-dependent and at lower densities than currently exists in the region. But it consumes less land overall than the High-Speed Rail scenario, and it encroaches less on prime farmland, primarily because the improved highways provide a growth magnet that is removed from the core of prime farmland in the Valley.

All four scenarios are speculative and none should be taken as an accurate prediction of future growth in the San Joaquin Valley. But they illustrate the different directions growth might take, and they highlight the kinds of choices the San Joaquin Valley will likely have to make to assure a prosperous and livable future. We now turn to the question of whether Valley residents are ready to make such choices.

6. Public Opinion and Policy Choices for the San Joaquin Valley

If the San Joaquin Valley experiences significant urban growth in the next 40 years, as our model suggests, it will be challenged in almost every aspect of its economic, social, political, and cultural life. Large areas will no longer be agricultural. Urbanization will call forth a new economic basis for employment and income; it will require huge expenditures on infrastructure of every kind; it will exacerbate such problems as air pollution, traffic congestion, water supply, and land-use conflict; and it will transform the political structure.

We do not argue that urbanization in the form that has occurred elsewhere in California is simply negative. All of these changes, and more, have been observed with mixed results in such areas as the San Fernando Valley, the Inland Empire, and the Sacramento Valley. All four scenarios presented here have both positive and negative implications for the future of the Valley and its residents. Because the San Joaquin Valley stands on the edge of such dramatic change, it represents that rare instance when we can anticipate the massive growth and change on the horizon and use the lessons from urbanization of regions to face the challenges ahead. The four scenarios represent different directions that the Valley could take if different regional policy decisions are made, although none can be viewed as a literal prediction of the future.

Issues in Urban Development
The main questions at hand are:

- What policy choices might be made now, looking toward the long-term future?

- What is the likelihood that the Valley might be able to mobilize to choose policies that would make its urbanization result in a better quality of life for its residents?

Neither of these questions can be answered simply. Consider the issue of alternative policies. Some advocates would seek to stop or slow growth to preserve current structures and lifestyles. Whether for reasons of environmental conservation, belief in the sanctity or economic necessity of agriculture, or to preserve immediate neighborhood quality, such policy proposals are unlikely to be effective, especially in their extreme forms. The forces of population growth and its attendant physical development have proved to be extremely powerful in California for more than 100 years. The San Fernando and Santa Clara Valleys provide clear examples of the power of urban population growth.

At the same time, those who argue that the current mode of development is both desirable and the best that can be done are also sending a simplistic message. No urban development occurs without public policy, whether explicit or implicit. Historically, federal, state, and local governments have enabled or impeded development in a multitude of ways, ranging from the direct provision of infrastructure, such as freeways and water supply, to the regulation of construction for any number of reasons. In part, public action has responded to the fact that development usually has many supporters—notably landowners, developers, builders, infrastructure providers, and others who benefit from it economically—as well as opponents.

This is especially true in rural areas on the edges of major urban areas, where massive new development has often occurred in the United States. Essentially, development consists of the transformation of agricultural, forest, or wildland areas into low-density urban uses— precisely the kind of transformation that our Accommodating Urban Development scenario suggests. In a rural society, those in favor of development are more likely to be well financed and able to move political decisions in their preferred directions. Furthermore, the view of development as progress is more likely to match the conservative tendency of rural populations, even though it implies massive transformations. In consequence, the discourse about development is often hostile to regulation and planning in the development process, except insofar as it supports development. It is only after development has taken its course and has revealed new problems that an organized and articulate constituency with the financial and political resources to affect decisions about regulation is likely to arise.

Past and Current Regionalism Efforts in the San Joaquin Valley

California has always struggled over reconciling the regional nature of growth issues with the desire for local control over development. For most of the last half-century, the result has been "fractured regionalism," in which "control over the policy areas that constitute growth management—infrastructure, environmental, and land use planning— was dispersed among different levels of government, none of them organized at the metropolitan scale in most cases" (Barbour, 2002).

Although more regional initiatives have emerged in California in recent years, these efforts have tended to fall into two categories—those mandated by federal environmental law and those encouraged by mutual self-interest. The federal Endangered Species Act, for example, has stimulated the creation of "habitat conservation plans," which in the California context have sometimes served as conservation-based regional land-use plans guiding where development will occur and where it will not. The changes in federal transportation policy that began with the passage of the Intermodal Surface Transportation Policy Act (ISTEA) in 1991 have given more power to metropolitan-level transportation decisionmakers and stimulated more regional thinking in that regard throughout California.

Nonetheless, a gap remains on many growth issues, especially housing and the jobs-housing balance, where there is no strong state or federal regulation and little perception of mutual self-interest in the part of local governments (Fulton et al., 1998). In housing, for example, regional councils of government (which in the Valley operate at the county-level not at the broader regional level) attempt to implement the state's housing element law, but the law does not appear to be strong enough to induce local governments to pursue regional housing interests and its effectiveness is not clear (Lewis, 2003). The efforts of the California Center for Regional Leadership to build regional consortia fall into the same general category, although they are even more voluntaristic and nongovernmental.

Historically, San Joaquin Valley leaders have shown a powerful willingness to work regionally toward mutually beneficial goals. The most obvious example of this pattern was the Central Valley Project, which was promoted by agricultural landowners for decades before its construction by the federal government in the 1930s. In the last decade, the perception of the San Joaquin Valley as a region with a common set of growth-related issues has increased, and various governmental agencies and stakeholders in the region have attempted to grapple with regional issues in a new way. In most cases, however, these regional processes and the stakeholder groups involved have been fairly circumscribed either in scope or in geographical range.

Perhaps the most highly publicized regional effort is the CALFED process, a consortium of state and federal agencies focused on resolving the conflicting economic and environmental issues in the Sacramento Delta area. CALFED has a potentially huge effect on the San Joaquin Valley because of its relationship to the San Joaquin River and the diversion of water throughout the Valley. CALFED efforts, for example, may eventually lead to retirement of considerable agricultural land in the San Joaquin Valley for environmental purposes. A somewhat related effort has been the state's Delta Protection Commission, a five-county commission that includes San Joaquin County and seeks to protect environmentally sensitive land in the Sacramento Delta through coordinated local planning efforts. Unlike the Coastal Commission, the Delta Protection Commission has no regulatory power, but recent legislative efforts have suggested strengthening the commission's power.

Perhaps the most innovative attempt to deal with regional issues has been the Inter-Regional Partnership (IRP), a coordinated effort among the councils of governments representing five counties—the two major Bay Area spillover counties (Stanislaus and San Joaquin) and three significant job-generating counties in the Bay Area (Alameda, Contra Costa, and Santa Clara). This partnership is also long on coordination and short on actual power, but it has highlighted jobs-housing balance issues in the two regions and has provided the basis for a state policy discussion about these issues. The IRP is gradually gaining credibility in Sacramento and could provide a vehicle for dealing with regional jobs-housing matters.

One of the most wide-ranging regional agency efforts in the San Joaquin Valley is the regulatory program of the San Joaquin Valley Air Pollution Control District (APCD), which is virtually the only government agency that operates at the scale of the eight counties. Traditionally, air districts such as the APCD—which operate under the state implementation effort of the federal Clean Air Act—have steered clear of land-use issues, as they have focused on stationary sources of air pollution. However, the APCD is currently considering passage of a fee on development projects to offset the air pollution those projects cause (Weiser, 2004).

In addition, a series of other miscellaneous efforts, both governmental and nongovernmental, have emerged in the last decade. The Great Valley Center, founded in Modesto in 1997, seeks to highlight regional issues in the larger 18-county Central Valley region. A diverse group of stakeholders in the Fresno area, including builders, farmers, and "smart growth" advocates, has formed the Fresno Growth Alternatives Alliance to deal with growth issues there. And in 2002, President Bush and Agriculture Secretary Ann Veneman (from Modesto) formed the Central San Joaquin Valley Interagency Task Force to coordinate federal efforts in the Valley. The task force covers seven of the eight San Joaquin Valley counties, excluding San Joaquin.

These initiatives all suggest an increasing interest in dealing with regional issues associated with growth, but most land-use power still lies in the hands of the region's cities and counties. Thus, true regional coordination remains elusive.

Growth Policy Options for the San Joaquin Valley

This report describes the potential effect of four growth scenarios that are based on different policy assumptions—principally the protection of farmland and the possibility of making different types of transportation investments. As stated above, these scenarios were not meant to be literal forecasts of the future or prescriptive. Rather, they provide a broad-brush prediction of general outcomes that might result from different alternative futures.

Nevertheless, it is important to assess how public policy could be informed by these scenarios, and whether and how changes in public policy might bring about a more desirable future than the Accommodating Urban Development scenario that would occur if historical trends, including massive subsidies to development, simply move forward.

To answer these questions, it is important to step back and examine the underlying determinants of growth that are embedded in the four scenarios. In general, they are

- Transportation investments,
- Conservation of nonurbanized land, and
- Land-use density.

All of these three drivers can be manipulated by public policy— although whether that manipulation is successful in achieving the desired policy goals depends a great deal on both the clarity of the goal, the strength of the public policy tools used, and the consistency with which those tools are implemented. The first driver, transportation, is shaped mostly by public investments. The second is shaped by a combination of public investments and regulation, and the third is shaped largely by regulation. We might add a fourth category that applies mostly to preservation and land use, namely, the broad spectrum of financial inducements that government agencies provide to private landowners as a way to stimulate, discourage, or shape urban growth, although this category does not appear explicitly in our model. We will now deal with each of these in the context of the San Joaquin Valley.

Transportation Investments

Two of the four scenarios laid out in this report attempt to estimate the consequences of different types of infrastructure investments— the proposed high-speed rail system and a selected set of highway improvements (mostly east-west), many of which seem likely to be constructed eventually. The results suggest that large-scale transportation improvements are among the most powerful drivers of growth patterns at a regional level.

Whether such investments can be used to overtly influence future urbanization patterns in the San Joaquin Valley is highly questionable. Transportation investment decisions are often made at the regional or state level, but they are rarely made with the goal of managing regional growth in mind. Usually they are designed to improve a statewide transportation route, or to solve a local or subregional traffic problem. At the county level, only Contra Costa County has a policy in place that ties transportation funds to a growth management strategy. Attempts to tie transportation investments to a growth strategy at the state level have failed repeatedly.

It is therefore unlikely that future transportation investments at the state level will be tied to a growth management strategy. In California, additional transportation funding for projects of regional significance tends to be shaped at the county level in the form of local option transportation sales taxes. Few, if any, of the eight San Joaquin Valley counties have enacted such taxes at present. Meanwhile, the high-speed rail project is moving forward slowly and may or may not be built eventually. But most planning around it has been focused on the need for a statewide high-speed rail system rather than on its possible effect on urbanization patterns in the Central Valley.

Conservation of Nonurbanized Land

One scenario used as its driver the possibility of protecting all farmland classified by the state as prime farmland. It is unlikely that any public land acquisition or protection strategy will seek to uniformly protect prime farmland, as the scenario assumed. However, a wide variety of land acquisition and protection efforts are under way all over the San Joaquin Valley. Some seek to purchase development rights for farmland; others seek to buy undeveloped land for environmental purposes.

There is little question, for example, that CALFED implementation efforts will ultimately lead to state or federal purchase of significant farmland in the southern part of the Valley to retire it from production and improve environmental conditions. Although all these efforts will shape urban growth in some way, the general trend in land acquisition and protection nationwide is not consciously coordinated with efforts to manage growth, either at a local or a regional level (Hollis and Fulton, 2002). As with transportation, coordinating these land conservation efforts in the service of an overall growth strategy is certainly possible, but judging by the record, it is unlikely.

Land-Use Density

Our scenarios varied widely in the implied density of future urban development, which is due in large part to the presumed density of individual development projects. However, most actual land-use regulatory power is in the hands of local cities and counties, and local jurisdictions in California are under no obligation to consider broader regional issues in exercising that power. Even when local governments engage in more sophisticated growth management mechanisms—such as urban growth boundaries, promotion of "infill" or high-density development, or population and housing restrictions—they do so in pursuit of local goals and with little concern for regional problems. In fact, these efforts sometimes exacerbate regional problems rather than solve them (Glickfeld and Levine, 1992).

On the other hand, many environmental regulations have an indirect—and sometimes direct—effect on how land is used. The best examples here are the federal and state Endangered Species Acts, which sometimes lead to a conservation planning process requiring that landowners set aside (and public agencies buy) land that would otherwise be available for development. In addition, the environmental review process required under the California Environmental Quality Act often leads to "mitigation measures" that affect the shape and scale of urban development, at least at the level of the individual development project. Although the federal- and state-driven conservation plans sometimes take regional ecosystem issues into account, none of these tools deal with growth patterns on a regional level.

Financial Inducements That Can Shape Growth Patterns

In addition, public policy in California provides a variety of financial inducements that seek to shape growth patterns or have the inadvertent effect of doing so. For example, the Williamson Act, which is widely used throughout the San Joaquin Valley, seeks to discourage landowners from developing their property by allowing them to enter into rolling 10-year contracts that provide them with lower property taxes. Redevelopment efforts seek to provide private developers with financial subsidies to locate their investments in blighted urban areas. Also, it is common California practice—widely used in some parts of the Valley—to require that developers shoulder some or most of the burden of infrastructure cost on individual projects. This financial burden often has the effect of creating somewhat denser developments, as the developers seek to save on infrastructure costs.

Development fees such as those proposed by the APCD can also serve to alter growth patterns as well. These fees can be a deterrent to development in some cases; in others, they can induce developers to pursue "high end" development; and in still others they can encourage the construction of more infrastructure than would otherwise be constructed by providing a new funding source for them.

Examples from Other Regions and Other States

Most of the tools described above affect a region's growth patterns, but often that effect is a by-product of some narrower policy goal, such as improved traffic flow, protection of natural resources, or economic development. Of course, it is possible to use these tools for the explicit purpose of managing regional growth, either by limiting or geographically directing the growth's "footprint."

However, such efforts usually require a policy commitment at the state level, especially for regulation. Such a commitment has been made in a few cases in California and the United States. Perhaps the best examples in California are the Coastal Commission and the Tahoe Regional Planning Agency, a bi-state agency between California and Nevada, each of which regulates land use at the regional level for environmental protection purposes. But in these and other cases, including the Adirondack Park Agency, the impetus for growth management generally does not come from the local residents but from powerful constituencies, such as environmentalists, who assert a stake in the region.

A few other states have engaged in growth policy at the state level. Oregon has a well-known "top-down" system of regional planning requiring that each metropolitan area create an urban growth boundary. Maryland has a budget-driven system in which state budget priorities are based on a statewide strategy to encourage growth in some areas and encourage conservation in others.

These are the exceptions rather than the rule, however. By and large, the ability to plan effectively for urban development, in a context where local government dominates the decision process, is likely to depend critically on the kind of place in which development is happening. As we stated above, historical experience suggests that places on the urban periphery are politically, ideologically, and culturally less likely to be open to the prospect of shaping development in the interest of longer-term and wider geographic constituencies.

As growth accelerates, however, things may change. One interesting example is Riverside County, a large, fast-growing, and politically conservative area in inland Southern California that has undergone growth pressures similar to those faced by the Bay Area spillover counties of Stanislaus and San Joaquin Counties. Confronted with many endangered species issues, Riverside County faced intense pressure from the state and federal government to prepare a multispecies conservation plan. Faced also with additional growth and more residents commuting to Los Angeles, Orange, and San Diego Counties, the county needed to prepare a transportation plan calling for the creation of several new transportation corridors.

Instead of piecemealing these efforts, the county undertook a multiyear, multimillion-dollar effort to coordinate planning for wildlife preserves, transportation, and—at least in the unincorporated areas—land use as well. The result is the Riverside County Integrated Project, which provides the backbone for both the "green" and the transportation infrastructure of the county in the face of rapid future growth.

The Riverside County experience was not perfect—among other things, the county land-use plan was not coordinated with the land-use plans of the cities—but it could provide a model. Riverside is a very large county—larger than the three Bay spillover counties combined and almost as large as Kern County—and so the issues dealt with in the

Integrated Project were regional in nature. However, it is only one county, whereas the San Joaquin Valley encompasses eight counties in a much larger geographical area.

The foregoing discussion suggests that the San Joaquin Valley certainly has the public policy tools at its disposal to deal with regional growth issues. However, it is unclear whether the Valley has the political will or even the cultural or ideological inclination to use those tools in a coordinated way. Given all these trends, is it possible for the San Joaquin Valley—or its subregions—to create a regional approach to managing growth that respects the political and cultural patterns of the Valley and also effectively addresses the looming regional problems?

Awareness of Development Issues in the San Joaquin Valley

The history and current character of the San Joaquin Valley suggest that it may not recapitulate the standard process of urbanization so often seen in California. As a result of almost 50 years of debate over environmental issues, together with the rise of mass communications on a scale never previously seen, people are more likely to have access to information about urban issues now than ever before. The regional issues that we discuss in this report—farmland conservation, transportation investments, and different kinds of urban growth—have been publicized and debated more vigorously in the Valley than in most traditionally rural areas undergoing urbanization pressure. However, the Valley's residents are also bombarded with conflicting messages on an unprecedented scale.

Although the debate has been widespread, it is not always easy to assess what the Valley's residents know and think about regional growth issues. One source of public opinion is the PPIC series of Statewide Surveys in the Central Valley, which have been carried out, in conjunction with the Great Valley Center, since 1999 (Baldassare, various years). From those surveys, it is possible to gain a picture of public opinion in the population of the San Joaquin Valley—and, in so doing, to assess the prospects for regional thinking and regional policymaking.[1]

Generally, the Valley's population is very positive about its communities as places to live (Table 6.1). Over the last five years, surveys have revealed that over 70 percent of respondents rated their communities as excellent or good places to live.

Over 50 percent of Valley residents live in places that they see as small cities or towns, and they like where they live. There is no evidence that this pattern has been changing over time.

Although they are satisfied, Valley residents perceive serious problems. The proportion of respondents seeing things moving in the right direction fell from 64 percent to 56 percent over the five years of the surveys, with ratings of the economy as excellent or good falling from 49 percent to 35 percent. When asked for their opinion of the most important problem facing the Valley, most respondents named air pollution in four of the five years. The survey question was open-ended, which resulted in a very broad spectrum of answers. Yet in 2004, over 20 percent of respondents described air pollution as the most important.

Within the region, in 2004, there were substantial differences among areas—especially between the Bay Area–influenced north Valley and the

Table 6.1

San Joaquin Valley Residents' Ratings of Their Communities as Places to Live, 1999–2004

"Overall, how would you rate your city or community as a place to live? Would you say it is excellent, good, fair, or poor?"

| | Percentage of Respondents | | | | |
	1999	2001	2002	2003	2004
Excellent	23	24	26	25	26
Good	46	48	48	47	45
Fair	23	22	22	22	23
Poor	7	7	5	5	6

SOURCE: Baldassare (various years).

NOTE: Percentages may not sum to totals because of rounding.

---

[1]Although the survey covered the entire Central Valley, we have been able to break out a sample of over 1,000 respondents in the San Joaquin Valley.

agricultural south Valley. For the three northern counties, the most important issue was population growth and development, which was cited by 15 percent of respondents; air pollution was noted by 14 percent. In the southern five counties, air pollution was mentioned by 32 percent of respondents.

How residents see the relative scale of problems in the Valley is provided by the responses shown in Table 6.2.

This table summarizes a series of questions, each asking whether a specific issue was seen as a "big problem," "somewhat of a problem," or "not a problem in your part of the Central Valley." For simplicity in presentation, we show only the percentages seeing the issues as big problems over the five years of the surveys.

Eight issues were presented to respondents for their assessment: traffic congestion on freeways and major roads, availability of affordable housing, loss of farms and agricultural lands, air pollution, lack of

Table 6.2

San Joaquin Valley Residents Seeing the Issue as a Big Problem, 1999–2004

"I am now going to read you a list of problems other people have told us about. For each one, please tell me if you think this is a big problem, somewhat of a problem, or not a problem in your part of the Central Valley."

	Percentage of Respondents Saying "Big Problem"				
	1999	2001	2002	2003	2004
Lack of opportunities for well-paying jobs	(a)	41	48	51	—
Air pollution	26	29	39	48	53
Loss of farms and agricultural lands	26	35	39	44	39
Traffic congestion	14	22	24	35	35
Availability of affordable housing	—	23	26	33	—
Population growth and development	18	23	24	27	27
Water quality	—	—	23	25	23
Water supply	—	—	16	21	—

SOURCE: Baldassare (various years).

aCertain observations are unavailable because of periodic changes in the survey design.

opportunities for well-paying jobs, population growth and development, and water quality and supply. Not all issues were asked about in every year. Nonetheless, the responses reveal consistent patterns.

The most striking feature of Table 6.2 is the overall growth in perception of problems as major over these years. Every issue, except water quality, was seen as a big problem by a growing proportion of residents over the five years, although the peak proportions varied over time. In some instances, notably traffic congestion and air pollution, the increases were dramatic. Evidently, people's awareness of issues has risen far more sharply than the problems themselves in this short period, with the exception of the lack of well-paying jobs, which clearly is related to the recession. For whatever reasons, perhaps including the publicity given to surveys such as these, people are both aware of and concerned about major issues related to development.

Attitudes Toward Responsibility and Policy

If Valley residents are increasingly aware of issues, what do they think about their public institutions that have responsibility for dealing with those issues, and what do they see as ways to address them? Are they ready to take direct responsibility for dealing with problems? Opinion polls must be regarded with caution on such questions, but they can provide valuable indications of attitudes toward policy.

When asked about their satisfaction with the performance of their city and county in solving problems, only about 40 percent rated them as excellent or good, and over 50 percent saw them as fair or poor, with little change between 1999 and 2004. On the other hand, when asked about services, such as local parks, streets, police, and schools, respondents tended to be more positive, with ratings of excellent or good by 60 to 70 percent of respondents for most services, and little change over time. Apparently, Valley residents are skeptical about their government institutions' ability to solve problems, even while satisfied with what they get from them in services.

That said, what might residents be willing to do to address the problems that they see now? Their views are mixed but indicate a willingness to act. To the most direct question—would they be willing to raise the sales tax by 1 percent to fund city services?—55 percent were in favor and 42 percent were opposed in 2003. This shows strong underlying support but not enough to pass such a tax, which would usually require a two-thirds vote in favor. For school funding, however, which they evidently regard as a state responsibility, those percentages were almost exactly reversed. Asked about actions that they themselves might take to counter air pollution, over half stated that they would be willing to take public buses or transit, even if it would be less convenient, and over three-quarters stated their willingness to drive a more fuel-efficient and low-polluting vehicle. We might be skeptical about these numbers, especially in light of the fact that fewer than half were willing to see tougher air pollution regulations, especially if they would be more costly or hurt the economy.

These responses do not tell us what people in the Valley think about the issue of who should take care of problems in the future. Reinforcing the equivocal nature of their attitudes to intervention, when respondents were asked in 2003 which level of government should have primary responsibility for setting air quality standards—the federal government, the state, a regional air resources board, or local government—the largest single response was local government (29%), followed by a regional board (26%), the state (24%), and the federal government (12%). Clearly, there is no clear-cut sense of the right institutional structure to do the job.

Valley residents seem to hold ambivalent views about how to address the future. Asked in 2004 about their views on how local governments should plan for future land use and growth, about 70 percent responded that local governments should work together for a common regional plan, whereas 25 percent took the view that governments should work independently and each have its own plan. This result indicates potential support for regional solutions, albeit worked out by local negotiation.

In the 2003 survey, however, when asked which was closer to their views—local elected officials providing leadership in planning or local voters making most of the important decisions at the ballot box—respondents resoundingly chose the ballot box over local elected officials by 75 to 22 percent. It could be argued that Valley residents want the final say on regional issues; but without a larger state framework that establishes when a regional majority might override local views, such a solution would be generally unworkable.

Another approach might emphasize nonpartisan organizations intended to bring together governments, businesses, and citizens' groups. Asked about this possibility, over half of respondents agreed that such an effort would be very important, and a further 34 percent felt that it would be somewhat important.

Conclusion

Although they are not intended to be literal depictions of what the future might bring, the four scenarios presented in this report suggest that conscious policy choices on a regional level could have a powerful effect on the San Joaquin Valley's growth patterns. Most dramatically, the accommodating growth scenario would create a much more fragmented and sprawling development pattern than the other alternatives. Although we have not examined the possible negative effects of these development patterns in detail, it is likely that the potential for such effects could be altered if the development pattern is altered on a regional basis.

Whether the San Joaquin Valley has the capacity to alter that development pattern is open to question. Tools for urban policy exist, although few have been tried in the Valley. As we stated above, intense urbanization in a traditionally rural area often reveals an apparent conflict between the growing problems associated with urbanization and the political culture of the region. On the one hand, history suggests that more forward-looking planning and proactive regional policy approaches would help an urbanizing region deal with the negative consequences of growth. On the other hand, a traditionally rural area is less likely to be receptive to strong planning approaches.

The PPIC survey evidence suggests that, in contrast to residents of many rural areas experiencing urbanization, residents of the San Joaquin Valley are quite aware of the issues that urbanization will bring. However, they by no means agree on the best way to proceed; indeed, they hold views that may be mutually incompatible and may make concerted action very difficult.

Without leadership and effort, the most likely outcome over the coming decades will be the creation of a complex, almost continuous city along the eastern side of the Valley. The history of urbanization in California suggests this outcome, and it is what most of our scenarios forecast, although with varying degrees of fragmentation.

Many stakeholders would see such a prospect as acceptable and even desirable—which is, of course, part of the reason it is the likely "default" pattern of urbanization. But, as we stated above, the scale of the San Joaquin Valley, the relatively early stage of major urbanization, and the awareness of the potential problems present an unusual opportunity. Furthermore, this opportunity is intertwined with the social and economic aspects of the urbanization process that we described in Chapter 2.

At the same time that the landscape of the San Joaquin Valley is urbanizing dramatically, so too is its economy. The role of agriculture in the Valley's economy is changing. Farming remains the foundation of the economy, but agricultural employment is gradually shifting from the farms themselves to the cities, where secondary agricultural sectors are gaining employment. At the same time, the service sector is growing, but no new, strong economic foundation for the Valley's urban economy has yet emerged.

Large segments of the population remain relatively poor and uneducated, a legacy of the Valley's agricultural history. With farm jobs declining, this population is now mostly in cities—and, because of the economic transitions noted above, this population has no obvious path toward upward mobility.

Thus, the social, economic, and physical urbanization challenges of the San Joaquin Valley are interrelated in ways that are relevant to the future growth scenarios that we have outlined here. Would the Accommodating Urban Development scenario create a disjunction between development patterns driven by low-density homeownership and urban decay issues resulting from social conditions? If a prime farmland conservation scenario were pursued, what type of agricultural economy should it be designed to support, and which agricultural land should be targeted? If some type of transportation scenario were pursued—one including, perhaps, high-speed rail, highway improvements, or a combination of the two—what economic strategy should these policy choices be designed to support?

Although this report may not describe the exact shape of the Valley's urban future, the challenges it depicts are credible and likely. Whether the population of the Valley and its political leaders are able and willing to grasp the opportunity will be a key issue for the coming decades.

Appendix
The SLEUTH Model

SLEUTH is a cellular automata (CA) urban growth model that has been widely used to model urbanization throughout various regions of the United States and the world (Jantz, Goetz, and Shelley, 2004; Yang and Lo, 2003; Esnard and Yang, 2002; Silva and Clarke, 2002; Clarke, Hoppen, and Gaydos, 1997). SLEUTH can model urban/nonurban dynamics as well as urban land-use dynamics, although the latter has not been widely used, presumably because of limitations in gathering consistently classified land-use data. Its dual ability has led to the development of two subcomponents within the framework of the model: The urban growth model (UGM) models urban/nonurban growth, and the other models land-use change dynamics (Deltatron). Regardless of which subcomponent is used, the model has the same calibration routine. The input of land-use data during calibration activates the Deltatron part of SLEUTH.

Required Data

SLEUTH requires topographic data in the form of slope and hillshade maps, although the hillshade data are used only for visualization and do not play a role in determining model outputs. Land-use data with consistent classification for two time periods are needed to implement the Deltatron submodel. They are not necessary to simulate urban growth, however, but are recommended. An exclusion layer is used to place constraints on urban growth. Through this layer, a user can specify where urban growth is allowed and where it is prohibited. This layer can also be weighted so that "resistance" to growth can be put in place in an attempt to slow or alter the rate of urbanization. Urban extent data are critical and necessary for this model. Four temporal layers are needed to show urban areas at different points in time. These maps serve as the control points, against which the model is calibrated, and a goodness of fit is determined. The last layer required for using SLEUTH is transportation. Historical maps of the transportation network show its evolution over time. Because different types of roads attract urban growth in different ways, roads in the transportation map are classified according to access. Roads classified with a value of 100 are generally high-access roads such as freeways, interstates, and state routes. Primary local roads are given a weight of 50, and secondary roads are classified as 25. The creation of these input maps is typically done within a GIS and then they are converted to GIFS which are the actual data used in the model.

Urban Growth Model

Calibration of SLEUTH produces a set of five parameters (coefficients) that describe an individual growth characteristic and when combined with other characteristics can describe several different growth processes. For this model, the transition rules between time periods are uniform across space and are applied in a nested set of loops. The outermost loop executes each growth period, and an inner loop executes growth rules for a single year. Transition rules and initial conditions of urban areas and land use at the start time are integral to the model because of how the calibration process adapts the model to the local environment. Clarke and Gaydos (1998) describe the initial condition set as the "seed" layer, from which growth and change occur one cell at a time, each cell acting independently of the others, until patterns emerge during growth and the "organism" learns more about its environment. The transition rules involve taking a cell at random, investigating the spatial properties of its neighborhood, and then urbanizing the cell, depending on probabilities influenced by other local characteristics (Clarke, Hoppen, and Gaydos, 1997). Five coefficients (with values of 0 to 100) control the behavior of the system and are predetermined by the user at the outset of every model run (Candau, 2000; Clarke and Gaydos, 1998; Clarke, Hoppen, and Gaydos, 1997). The parameters drive the four transition rules that simulate four types of urban growth: spontaneous (of suitable slope and distance from existing centers), diffusive (new growth centers), organic (infill and edge growth), and road-influenced (a function of road gravity and density). These parameters are:

1. *Diffusion*—Determines the overall dispersiveness nature of the outward distribution. This parameter controls the number of times that a pixel will be randomly selected for possible urbanization, and is calculated as

$$\text{diffusion value} = ((\text{diffusion coefficient} * 0.005) * \sqrt{((\text{number of rows})^2 + (\text{number of columns})^2})$$

This means that the maximum diffusion value will be half of the input image diagonal.

2. *Breed coefficient*—The likelihood that a newly generated detached settlement will start on its own growth cycle.

3. *Spread coefficient*—Controls how much contagion diffusion radiates from existing settlements.

4. *Slope resistance factor*—Influences the likelihood of development on steep slopes.

5. *Road gravity factor*—An attraction factor that draws new settlements toward and along roads.

Transition Rules

The five parameters control the four transition rules generated within SLEUTH: spontaneous, new spreading center, edge, and road-influenced growth. The transition rules are applied in the order of rules listed above.

Spontaneous Growth

Spontaneous growth, much as its name describes, determines the occurrence of random urbanization in the landscape. All cells that are not urban have some, albeit a small, chance of urbanizing at any time within the model. So the probability that a cell U, located in space at coordinates i,j, will become urbanized during the next time is defined as

$$U(i,j,t + 1) = f \,(\text{diffusion coefficient, slope coefficient}, \\ U\,(i,j,t), \text{random})$$

Here the diffusion coefficient determines the probability of urbanization and the slope coefficient determines the weighted probability of the local slope. The random term indicates that there is stochasticity in the process. At any time in the urbanization process, cells that are already urbanized and those in the excluded layer are prohibited from changing classes (Figure A.1). This process is described in pseudo code as follows:

```
F(diffusion coefficient, slope coefficient)
{
for (p < diffusion value)
{select pixel location (i,j) at random if ((i,j) is available for
urbanization) {
(i,j) = urban
new spreading center growth
} }
} end spontaneous growth
```

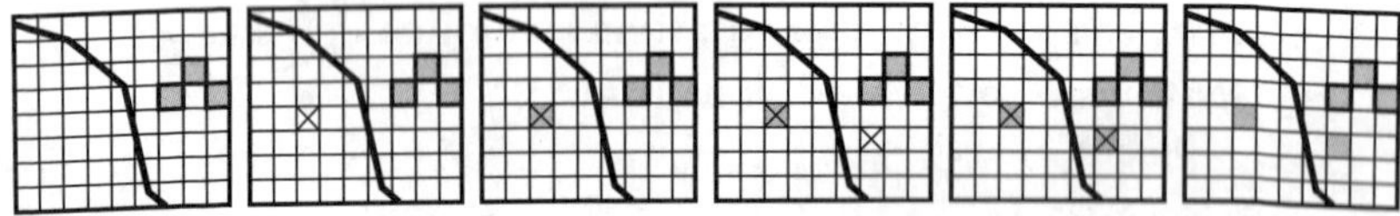

SOURCE: Gigalopolis webpage, www.ncgia.ucsb.edu/projects/gig.

Figure A.1—Process of Spontaneous Growth and Pseudo Code

New Spreading Centers

After establishing spontaneous urban growth on the landscape, SLEUTH attempts to turn some of the newly urbanized cells into spreading centers. This is done largely through the breed parameter, which defines the probability that each newly urbanized cell, $U(i, j, t + 1)$ will become a spreading center, $U'(i, j, t + 1)$, if there are two or more neighbors that can be urbanized (Figure A.2):

$$U'(i, j, t+1) = f \text{ (breed coefficient, } U(i, j, t+1), \text{ random)}$$

This process is described in pseudo-code as follows:

F(breed coefficient, slope coefficient)

{

if (random_integer < *breed_coefficient*)

if (two neighborhood pixels are available for urbanization)

(i,j) neighbors = urban

} end new spreading center growth

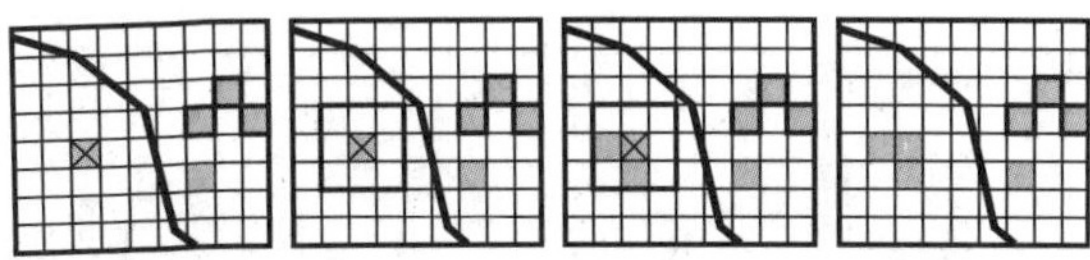

Figure A.2—Process of New Spreading Centers

Edge Growth

The most typical growth in urban systems is edge growth, whereby
nonurbanized areas adjacent to existing urban areas are transformed from
a nonurban into urban use. Edge growth attempts to capture these
dynamics by propagating growth from urban areas, whether preexisting
or those generated by spontaneous and new spreading centers growth. If
a nonurban cell has three or more urbanized neighbors, then it has a
probability of becoming urbanized that is defined by the spread
coefficient but with the constraints placed upon that cell by the slope
coefficient (Figure A.3):

U(i, j, t+1) = f (spread coefficient, slope coefficient,
U(i, j, t+1), U (k, l), random)

where (k, l) belongs to the nearest neighborhood if (i,j). This is
described in pseudo-code below.

Edge Growth:

F(spread coefficient, slope coefficient)

{

    for (all non-edge pixels *(i,j)*)

        if (*(i,j)* is urban) and (random_integer

< *spread_coefficient*)
   if (at least two urban neighbors exist)
   if (a randomly chosen, non-urban
      neighbor is available for urbanization)
   (i,j) neighbor = urban
} end edge growth

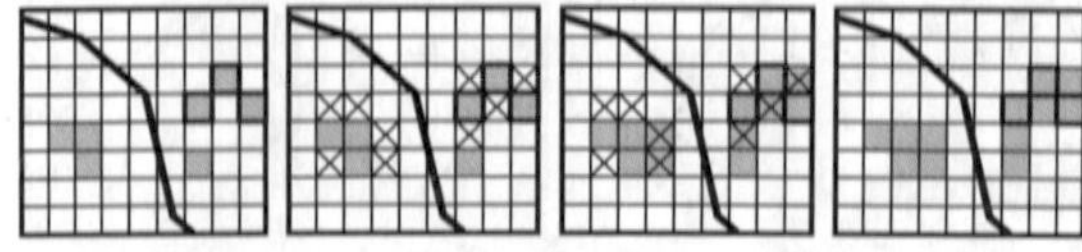

SOURCE: Gigalopolis webpage, www.ncgia.ucsb.edu/ projects/gig.

Figure A.3—Process of Edge Growth

Road-Influenced Growth

The last step in generating urban growth is to incorporate the influence of the transportation network in the urbanization process. This is done using the transportation input layers and the urbanization that was generated in the previous three steps. The breed coefficient determines the probability that newly urbanized cells (in the prior three steps) will be selected, and within their neighborhood the presence of a transportation route will be determined. If a portion of the transportation network is found within the radius of a particular cell (this radius is determined by the road gravity coefficient), then a temporary urban cell is placed at that point on the road closest to the already urbanized cell. This temporary cell then takes a random walk along the transportation network, where the number of steps is predetermined by the dispersion coefficient. The final location of the random walk is then considered as a new urban spreading nucleus. If a neighboring cell to the temporary urbanized cell (on the transportation network) can be urbanized, it will occur, as determined by a random draw among candidates. If two cells adjacent to this newly urbanized cell are also available for urbanization, that will happen (randomly picked among candidates). This process of road-influenced growth creating temporary urban cells along the transportation network is expressed through four steps:

$$U'(k, l, t + 1) = f'(U(i,j,t + 1), \text{road gravity coefficient}, R(m,n), \text{random})$$

Here i, j, k, l, m, and n are cell coordinates, with R (m,n) defining a road cell. The random walk is described as

$$U''(i, j, t + 1) = f''(U(k,l,t + 1), \text{diffusion coefficient}, R(m,n), \text{random})$$

In this equation, (i,j) are the road cells neighboring (k,l). The final location of the temporary random cell is defined as (p,q). Using this, the new urban spreading center is defined as

$$U'''(i, j, t + 1) = f'''(U(p,q,t + 1), R(m,n), \text{slope coefficient}, \text{random})$$

To add two adjacent urban cells to the spreading center, the equation is

$$U''''(i, j, t + 1) = f''''(U(p,q,t + 1), \text{slope coefficient}, \text{random})$$

In this case, (i, j) and (k,l) belong to the neighborhood of (p,q), These are the four steps that constitute the random walk of a cell through the transportation network.   The number of random walks that occur is determined by the breed coefficient.

The entire process of road influence growth can be described in pseudo-code as

```
F(breed coefficient, road gravity coefficient ,
diffusion coefficient, slope coefficient)
{
    for (p <= breed_coefficient)
    {
        road_gravity = value which is a function of
                image size and road_gravity_coefficient
        max_search = maximum distance, determined by
                road_gravity, for which a road pixel is searched
```

(i,j) = randomly selected pixel, urbanized within the
    current growth cycle
road_found = search outward from (i,j), up to
    max_search, for a road pixel
if (road_found)
{
    walk along the road, in randomly selected
        directions, for a number of steps determined
        by the road_value and the
        dispersion_coefficient
    if (a neighboring pixel is available for urbanization)
      (i,j) neighbor = urban
      if (two neighbors of the newly urban pixel
        are available for urbanization)
        two urban pixel neighbors = urban
  } } } end road-influenced growth

It is visualized in Figure A.4.

These four steps are the transition rules from nonurban to urban within the UGM portion of SLEUTH. At any time in the urbanization process, cells that are already occupied by existing urban areas or are

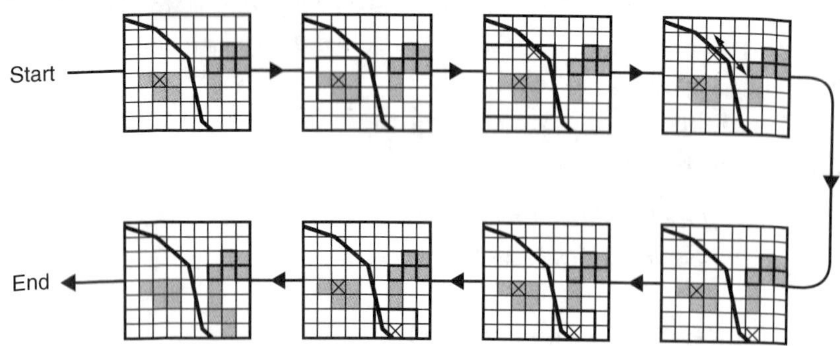

Figure A.4—Steps in Road-Influenced Growth: Searching the Cell Neighborhood for the Transportation Network, Taking a Random Walk, Establishing a Temporary Spreading Center, and Finally Establishing Urban Growth

excluded from development will by default cause a failure in the attempt to urbanize that particular cell. Implementation of these growth rules may in some cases lead to periods of excessively high or low growth rates. When this occurs, a second set of transition rules, known as self-modification, is implemented.

Self-Modification Rules

The process of urban growth is not a linear one. This is easily demonstrated by looking at the number of homes built over time. There are clear cycles of booms and busts, largely tied to urban and regional economics. To account for these cyclical periods of growth, SLEUTH has a second set of transition rules built in. Termed self-modification, these rules are implemented when there is a period of unusually high or low growth. If the growth rate (the sum the four growth processes) exceeds a critical high (specified in the scenario file that governs the model run), then breed, spread, and diffusion growth coefficients are increased by a value greater than one, and a "boom" cycle is initiated (Figure A.5). The opposite is also true. When the growth rate falls below a critical low, the breed spread and diffusion coefficients are multiplied by a value less than one, decreasing their value and creating a "bust-like" effect that causes urban growth to slow.

Model Calibration and Determining Goodness of Fit

By running the model in calibration mode, a set of control parameters is refined in the sequential "brute-force" calibration phases: coarse, fine, and final calibrations (Silva and Clarke, 2002), although other methods of calibration, including the use of genetic algorithms, have been suggested and tested (Goldstein, 2004). Initially the model was calibrated using hierarchical spatial resolutions, beginning with data of coarser resolution, narrowing the range of parameters that most accurately described the growth of the system, and then using a finer resolution to narrow the parameter values to one distinct set. Advances in computing power have allowed a more timely calibration, but it has been shown that using the hierarchical spatial resolution may lead to

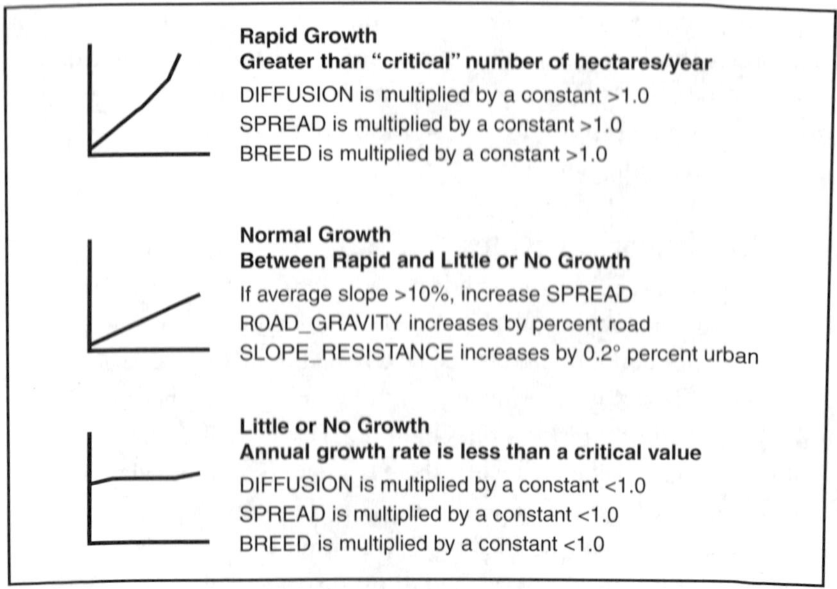

SOURCE: Gigalopolis webpage, www.ncgia.edu/projects/gig.

Figure A.5—Growth Patterns Under the Self-Modification Rules

parameter sets that do not as accurately describe the growth of the system as a calibration at full data resolution (Dietzel, 2004).

The coarse calibration begins with parsing the parameter space into five areas and using the values of 1, 25, 50, 75, and 100 for each of the five parameters. This gives 3,125 (5^5) parameter sets that are tested to determine within which range of parameters the one-parameter set that best describes the data is located. Results from the coarse calibration are examined to determine the goodness of fit for each parameter set. Narrowing of the parameter set can be based on a variety of different goodness of fit measures (Jantz, Goetz, and Shelley, 2004; Yang and Lo, 2003); no sole metric has been shown to be the most effective. Traditionally the Lee and Sallee (1970) metric has been used to determine which parameter sets best describe the replication of the historical datasets. Lee-Sallee is the ratio of the intersection and the union of the simulated and actual urban areas, but others including the *compare* statistic, and *population* statistics have been used. Table A.1

describes the 13 metrics that can be used to determine the goodness of fit of model calibration; they have a value range of 0 to 1, with 1 being a perfect fit.

Table A.1

Metrics That Can Be Used to Evaluate the Goodness of Fit of SLEUTH

Metric Name	Description
Product	All other scores multiplied together
Compare	Modeled population for final year/actual population for final year, or IF $P_{modeled > }P_{actual}\{ 1 - ($modeled population for final year/actual population for final year$)\}$
Pop	Least squares regression score for modeled urbanization compared to actual urbanization for the control years
Edges	Least squares regression score for modeled urban edge count compared to actual urban edge count for the control years
Clusters	Least squares regression score for modeled urban clustering compared to known urban clustering for the control years
Cluster size	Least squares regression score for modeled average urban cluster size compared to known average urban cluster size for the control years
Lee-Sallee	A shape index, a measurement of spatial fit between the model's growth and the known urban extent for the control years
Slope	Least squares regression of average slope for modeled urbanized cells compared to average slope of known urban cells for the control years
% urban	Least squares regression of percentage of available pixels urbanized compared to the urbanized pixels for the control years
X-mean	Least squares regression of average x_values for modeled urbanized cells compared to average x_values of known urban cells for the control years
Y-mean	Least squares regression of average y_values for modeled urbanized cells compared to average y_values of known urban cells for the control years
Rad	Least squares regression of average radius of the circle which encloses the urban pixels
F-Match	A proportion of goodness of fit across land use classes $\{ \#\_modeled\_LU$ correct$/(\#_modeled_LU$ correct $+ \#\_modeled\_LU$ wrong$)\}$

After determining the parameter set that best fits the historical data, a range of values around that set of parameters is selected and the calibration is run again. The goodness of fit of the second calibration is evaluated, and an even narrower range of parameters is selected. The best fitting parameters from this third calibration are then the parameters used in forecasting urban growth and land-use change.

Data Used in Modeling Future Development in the San Joaquin Valley

Data for modeling urban development were compiled from digital and paper cartographic sources.[1] Historical snapshots of urban extent in the San Joaquin Valley were the most important data needed to project future urban development. Urbanization was treated as a cumulative process, in which an area once urbanized could not be deurbanized. In looking at the historical urban growth trends in the San Joaquin Valley, urban extent data were compiled from 1940 to 2000 (Table A.2). Before beginning in on the discussion of the data used in this modeling, it is important to recall our definition of "urban" in this report. For the remainder of this report, the term "urban" will refer to:

> Land occupied by structures with a building density of at least 1 unit to 1.5 acres, or approximately 6 structures to a 10-acre parcel. This land is used for residential, industrial, commercial, construction, institutional, public administration, railroad and other transportation yards, cemeteries, airports, golf courses, sanitary landfills, sewage treatment, water control structures, and other developed purposes (http://www.consrv.ca.gov/DLRP/fmmp/).

The process of "urbanization" refers to the transformation of any other land-use type (field, forest, swamp, etc.) to one of those listed above. It is also important to note that the results presented are not what will happen but what might happen in the future. As with any forecast, there is an amount of uncertainty involved.

USGS data provided urban extent for 1940, 1954, 1962, and 1974 at 100m spatial resolution. Earlier work on the Central Valley by the

---

[1]The U.S. Geological Survey (USGS), the FMMP, the California Department of Water Resources (DWR), the California Department of Transportation, and the California Spatial Information Library.

USGS and Great Valley Center, entitled "Preliminary Assessment of Urban Growth in California's Central Valley" (http://ceres.ca.gov/calsip/cv/) used these data. Pre-1974 data were derived from 1:250,000 cartographic sources. 1974 data were from the first multispectral satellite images of California. Using the USGS National Land Cover Dataset (http://landcover.usgs.gov/), urban areas were drawn out of the land-use map of California for 1992 by selecting all of the urban land-use classes. These data were at $30m^2$ spatial resolution and resampled to $100m^2$ using the nearest neighbor method. Data on urban and developed land were extracted from FMMP's GIS database for 1984, 1986, 1988, 1990, 1992, 1994, 1996, 1998, and 2000. In each of these years, the minimum mapping unit of urban area was one building for one and a half acres. Department of Water Resources land-use surveys also provided information on historical urban extent. These were done at a county level and the years of survey are inconsistent for each county and do not occur at regular intervals. For some counties, more than one image was available and used; for other counties there was only one. These data were used to supplement the USGS and FMMP data at a more local scale. These were the datasets used in calibrating and forecasting SLEUTH.

Growth in the San Joaquin Valley has been driven by a variety of factors that need consideration when modeling and forecasting possible futures, including topographic features, the transportation network, and areas where growth is not readily allowed, including state and national parks. Topography for the San Joaquin Valley was generated using $30m^2$ digital elevation models in one-degree blocks from the California Spatial Information Library (www.gis.ca.gov). These blocks were downloaded and merged for all of California, then clipped to the extent of the San Joaquin Valley to create an elevation model, from which slope and a hillshade layer were derived and resampled to match the $100m^2$ resolution of the urban extent data. Recreation of the historical transportation network drew on the location of existing roads mapped by the California Department of Transportation (CalTrans) and projected in their GIS layer of functionally classified roads (http://www.dot.ca.gov/hq/tsip/TSIPGSC/library/libdatalist.htm). With this information as a base layer, roads were classified into high, medium, and low accessibility.

Historical state road maps for 1944, 1950, 1955, 1960, 1966, 1970, 1981, 1986, and 1990 existed in paper form from the Earth Science and Map Library of the University of California, Berkeley. Roads on the map were classified according to their accessibility, and then road segments were subtracted from the CalTrans GIS layer to recreate the historical map in digital format. All road maps, once in digital format were converted from lines to a grid format with a resolution of $100m^2$. Some areas are prohibited from development. These are mainly state and national parks, but may also include land owned by the Bureau of Land Management, U.S. Forest Service, and other government agencies. In modeling the future of the San Joaquin Valley, we made the assumption that all publicly owned lands in the San Joaquin Valley were excluded from future development. Data on the location of these lands, downloaded from the California Spatial Information Library (www.gis.ca.gov), were converted to a $100m^2$ resolution grid.

After assembly, the data for the entire San Joaquin Valley were clipped down to the county level, creating eight datasets, one for each county. These datasets were then calibrated.

Model Calibration Results

The eight counties of the San Joaquin Valley were each calibrated independently. An overall calibration was also tested, but it was found to be less effective. The following charts outline the calibration routines and results that were used to arrive at a final set of parameters then used in forecasting the four scenarios.

Defining Exclusion Layer for Scenarios

Using SLEUTH's exclusion layer, the four scenarios were implemented spatially to reflect resistance to urban development. Each scenario had different exclusion layers, leading to the different scenario results. Exclusion layers for each scenario were compiled at the scale of the San Joaquin Valley and then clipped down to the county level for forecasting.

Table A.2

Historical Sources of Data Used to Recreate the Urbanization of the San Joaquin Valley, 1940–2000

Year (s)	Source	Collection Method	Description	Resolution
1940	USGS	1:250,000 maps	Urban areas for all of San Joaquin Valley	$100m^2$
1954	USGS	1:250,000 maps	Urban areas for all of San Joaquin Valley	$100m^2$
1962	USGS	1:250,000 maps	Urban areas for all of San Joaquin Valley	$100m^2$
1974	USGS	MSS imagery	Urban areas for all of San Joaquin Valley	$30m^2$
1984	FMMP	Aerial photography	Urban and developed lands for all of San Joaquin Valley except Tulare and Kern Counties	1 building/1.5 acres
1986	FMMP	Aerial photography	Urban and developed lands for all of San Joaquin Valley except Kern County	1 building/1.5 acres
1986	DWR	Aerial photography	20 land-use classes for Fresno County	
1988	FMMP	Aerial photography	Urban and developed lands for all of San Joaquin Valley	1 building/1.5 acres
1988	DWR	Aerial photography	20 land-use classes for San Joaquin County	
1990	FMMP	Aerial photography	Urban and developed lands for all of San Joaquin Valley	1 building/1.5 acres
1990	DWR	Aerial photography	20 land-use classes for Kern County	
1991	DWR	Aerial photography	20 land-use classes for Kings County	
1992	FMMP	Aerial photography	Urban and developed lands for all of San Joaquin Valley	1 building/1.5 acres
1992	USGS	Landsat 5 imagery	Urban extracted from 1992 NLCD	$30m^2$
1993	DWR	Aerial photography	20 land-use classes for Tulare County	

Table A.2 (continued)

Year (s)	Source	Collection Method	Description	Resolution
1994	FMMP	Aerial photography	Urban and developed lands for all of San Joaquin Valley	1 building/1.5 acres
1994	DWR	Aerial photography	20 land-use classes for Fresno County	
1995	DWR	Aerial photography	20 land-use classes for Madera County	
1995	DWR	Aerial photography	20 land-use classes for Merced County	
1996	FMMP	Aerial photography	Urban and developed lands for all of San Joaquin Valley	1 building/1.5 acres
1996	DWR	Aerial photography	20 land-use classes for Kings County	
1996	DWR	Aerial photography	20 land-use classes for San Joaquin County	
1996	DWR	Aerial photography	20 land-use classes for Stanislaus County	
1998	FMMP	Aerial photography	Urban and developed lands for all of San Joaquin Valley	1 building/1.5 acres
1998	DWR	Aerial photography	20 land-use classes for Kern County	
1999	DWR	Aerial photography	20 land-use classes for Tulare County	
2000	FMMP	Aerial photography	Urban and developed lands for all of San Joaquin Valley	1 building/1.5 acres

Table A.3

Routines and Results for Calibrating SLEUTH for Fresno County, 1960–2000

Growth Parameters	Range	Step	Metric
Coarse: Monte Carlo iterations = 3			
Total no. of simulations = 3,125			
Diffusion	1–100	25	Lee-Sallee = 0.3081
Breed	1–100	25	
Spread	1–100	25	
Slope resistance	1–100	25	
Road gravity	1–100	25	
Fine: Monte Carlo iterations = 5			
Total no. of simulations = 4,320			
Diffusion	1–25	5	Lee-Sallee = 0.31201
Breed	1–25	5	
Spread	10–40	10	
Slope resistance	1–60	15	
Road gravity	50–100	10	
Final: Monte Carlo iterations = 7			
Total no. of simulations = 1,620			
Diffusion	1–5	1	Lee-Sallee = 0.31078
Breed	1–5	1	
Spread	28–32	2	
Slope resistance	58–62	2	
Road gravity	50–70	5	
Self-Modified Parameter Value (All Cases)			
Diffusion	2		
Breed	5		
Spread	58		
Slope resistance	41		
Road gravity	52		

Accommodating Urban Development

In the Accommodating Urban Development scenario, all publicly owned lands were given a value of 100. This value of 100 corresponded with the resistance to urban growth in these areas. The remainder of the San Joaquin Valley was given a value of 0, signifying no resistance to growth.

Table A.4

Routines and Results for Calibrating SLEUTH for Kern County, 1960–2000

Growth Parameters	Range	Step	Metric
Coarse: Monte Carlo iterations = 3			
Total no. of simulations = 3,125			
Diffusion	1–100	25	Lee-Sallee = 0.30439
Breed	1–100	25	
Spread	1–100	25	
Slope resistance	1–100	25	
Road gravity	1–100	25	
Fine: Monte Carlo iterations = 5			
Total no. of simulations = 2,592			
Diffusion	1–25	5	Lee-Sallee = 0.31299
Breed	1–25	5	
Spread	15–35	10	
Slope resistance	50–100	10	
Road gravity	1–30	10	
Final: Monte Carlo iterations = 7			
Total no. of simulations = 3,888			
Diffusion	1–5	1	Lee-Sallee = 0.31039
Breed	1–5	1	
Spread	28–32	2	
Slope resistance	50–60	2	
Road gravity	20–30	2	
Self-Modified Parameter Value			
(All Cases)			
Diffusion	2		
Breed	2		
Spread	58		
Slope resistance	46		
Road gravity	31		

Prime Farmland Conservation

All farmland designated prime in the San Joaquin Valley was given a value of 100, prohibiting urban growth in these areas. These were the areas identified as being prime farmland by the FMMP. All public lands previously excluded in the Accommodating Urban Development scenario were also excluded here. The rest of the San Joaquin Valley had a 0 resistance to growth.

Table A.5

**Routines and Results for Calibrating SLEUTH for Kings County,
1960–2000**

Growth Parameters	Range	Step	Metric
Coarse: Monte Carlo iterations = 3			
Total no. of simulations = 3,125			
Diffusion	1–100	25	Lee-Sallee = 0.20971
Breed	1–100	25	
Spread	1–100	25	
Slope resistance	1–100	25	
Road gravity	1–100	25	
Fine: Monte Carlo iterations = 5			
Total no. of simulations = 4,320			
Diffusion	1–25	5	Lee-Sallee = 0.29261
Breed	1–25	5	
Spread	1–25	5	
Slope resistance	20–60	10	
Road gravity	1–30	10	
Final: Monte Carlo iterations = 7			
Total no. of simulations = 2,160			
Diffusion	1–5	1	Lee-Sallee = 0.29684
Breed	1–5	1	
Spread	12–18	3	
Slope resistance	30–60	10	
Road gravity	1–20	5	
Self-Modified Parameter Value			
(All Cases)			
Diffusion	2		
Breed	2		
Spread	32		
Slope resistance	41		
Road gravity	22		

High-Speed Rail

The eight proposed rail stations were plotted, and then a 30-mile buffer
was drawn around them. Under this scenario, the area within this buffer
was twice as likely to be urbanized as the rest of the San Joaquin Valley.
Using these conditions, the area within the buffer was given a resistance
of 0. All publicly owned lands were excluded and given a value of 100,

Table A.6

Routines and Results for Calibrating SLEUTH for Madera County, 1960–2000

Growth Parameters	Range	Step	Metric
Coarse: Monte Carlo iterations = 3			
Total no. of simulations = 3,125			
Diffusion	1–100	25	Lee-Sallee = 0.2386
Breed	1–100	25	
Spread	1–100	25	
Slope resistance	1–100	25	
Road gravity	1–100	25	
Fine: Monte Carlo iterations = 5			
Total no. of simulations = 5,184			
Diffusion	1–25	5	Lee-Sallee = 0.27533
Breed	1–75	15	
Spread	1–25	5	
Slope resistance	75–100	5	
Road gravity	1–30	10	
Final: Monte Carlo iterations = 7			
Total no. of simulations = 3,456			
Diffusion	1–5	1	Lee-Sallee = 0.28645
Breed	1–5	1	
Spread	8–14	2	
Slope resistance	75–100	5	
Road gravity	1–30	10	
Self-Modified Parameter Value			
(All Cases)			
Diffusion	2		
Breed	2		
Spread	25		
Slope resistance	83		
Road gravity	21		

and the remaining area that was not within the buffer of the rail stations or publicly owned was given a value of 50.

Automobile-Oriented Managed Growth

A major goal in creating this scenario was to promote relatively compact growth along roads. The scenario had implemented five means to accomplish this. First, there was decreased development resistance of

Routines and Results for Calibrating SLEUTH for Merced County, 1960–2000

Growth Parameters	Range	Step	Metric
Coarse: Monte Carlo iterations = 3			
Total no. of simulations = 3,125			
Diffusion	1–100	25	Lee-Sallee = 0.26033
Breed	1–100	25	
Spread	1–100	25	
Slope resistance	1–100	25	
Road gravity	1–100	25	
Fine: Monte Carlo iterations = 5			
Total no. of simulations = 5,400			
Diffusion	1–25	5	Lee-Sallee = 0.26585
Breed	1–25	5	
Spread	15–35	5	
Slope resistance	1–100	25	
Road gravity	1–25	5	
Final: Monte Carlo iterations = 7			
Total no. of simulations = 7,776			
Diffusion	1–5	1	Lee-Sallee = 0.27036
Breed	1–5	1	
Spread	18–23	1	
Slope resistance	25–100	15	
Road gravity	1–25	5	
Self-Modified Parameter Value (All Cases)			
Diffusion	2		
Breed	2		
Spread	41		
Slope resistance	35		
Road gravity	15		

0 around the exits along Interstate 5. Second, the currently proposed foothills highway of California 65 would be built and would have a resistance to development of 0. Third, many of the major east-west routes in the San Joaquin Valley would be improved and widened, fostering development within a two-mile proximity to them, implemented by buffering these routes and giving them a resistance to development of 0. These routes are currently California state routes

Table A.8

Routines and Results for Calibrating SLEUTH for San Joaquin County, 1960–2000

Growth Parameters	Range	Step	Metric
Coarse: Monte Carlo iterations = 3			
Total no. of simulations = 3,125			
Diffusion	1–100	25	Lee-Sallee = 0.34829
Breed	1–100	25	
Spread	1–100	25	
Slope resistance	1–100	25	
Road gravity	1–100	25	
Fine: Monte Carlo iterations = 5			
Total no. of simulations = 6,480			
Diffusion	1–20	5	Lee-Sallee = 0.35244
Breed	1–25	5	
Spread	1–25	5	
Slope resistance	1–25	5	
Road gravity	15–75	5	
Final: Monte Carlo iterations = 7			
Total no. of simulations = 3,456			
Diffusion	1–10	2	Lee-Sallee = 0.33535
Breed	1–10	2	
Spread	20–30	2	
Slope resistance	1–30	10	
Road gravity	1–30	10	
Self-Modified Parameter Value			
(All Cases)			
Diffusion	2		
Breed	2		
Spread	54		
Slope resistance	1		
Road gravity	3		

(from north to south): 4, 120, 132, 140, 152, 180, 198, 41, 46, and 58. Fourth, all publicly owned lands would be excluded from development with a resistance value of 100. Finally, urbanization, although not unlikely in the remainder of the San Joaquin Valley, would be less likely, with a resistance value of 50.

Table A.9

**Routines and Results for Calibrating SLEUTH for Stanislaus County,
1960–2000**

Growth Parameters	Range	Step	Metric
Coarse: Monte Carlo iterations = 3			
Total no. of simulations = 3,125			
Diffusion	1–100	25	Lee-Sallee = 0.34441
Breed	1–100	25	
Spread	1–100	25	
Slope resistance	1–100	25	
Road gravity	1–100	25	
Fine: Monte Carlo iterations = 5			
Total no. of simulations = 4,500			
Diffusion	1–20	5	Lee-Sallee = 0.35935
Breed	1–20	5	
Spread	15–35	5	
Slope resistance	25–50	5	
Road gravity	50–100	10	
Final: Monte Carlo iterations = 7			
Total no. of simulations = 3,456			
Diffusion	1–10	2	Lee-Sallee = 0.34541
Breed	1–10	2	
Spread	20–30	5	
Slope resistance	40–50	2	
Road gravity	80–100	5	
Self-Modified Parameter Value			
(All Cases)			
Diffusion	2		
Breed	7		
Spread	54		
Slope resistance	29		
Road gravity	100		

Forecasting Scenarios and Compiling Results

Each scenario was forecast from 2000 to 2040, using SLEUTH in
the "predict" mode. Future urban growth was forecast through 100
Monte Carlo simulations for each county for each scenario. When all of
the county-level forecasts were complete, then they were merged within a
GIS to create one complete picture of the San Joaquin Valley for each
scenario. This was done for all scenarios. The results from the scenarios

Table A.10

Routines and Results for Calibrating SLEUTH for Tulare County, 1960–2000

Growth Parameters	Range	Step	Metric
Coarse: Monte Carlo iterations = 3			
Total no. of simulations = 3,125			
Diffusion	1–100	25	Lee-Sallee = 0.32958
Breed	1–100	25	
Spread	1–100	25	
Slope resistance	1–100	25	
Road gravity	1–100	25	
Fine: Monte Carlo iterations = 5			
Total no. of simulations = 2,160			
Diffusion	1–10	5	Lee-Sallee = 0.32786
Breed	1–15	5	
Spread	15–35	5	
Slope resistance	1–50	10	
Road gravity	1–50	10	
Final: Monte Carlo iterations = 7			
Total no. of simulations = 3,456			
Diffusion	1–3	1	Lee-Sallee = 0.31787
Breed	1–3	1	
Spread	20–25	1	
Slope resistance	1–50	10	
Road gravity	1–10	2	
Self-Modified Parameter Value			
(All Cases)			
Diffusion	2		
Breed	4		
Spread	45		
Slope resistance	1		
Road gravity	2		

were then used in analyzing a possible future for the San Joaquin Valley, as described in Chapters 3–5.

References

Baldassare, Mark, *Special Survey of the Central Valley*, Public Policy Institute of California, San Francisco, California (various years, 1999–2003).

Barbour, Elisa, *Metropolitan Growth Planning in California, 1900–2000*, Public Policy Institute of California, San Francisco, California, 2002.

Candau, Jeannette, "Calibrating a Cellular Automaton Model of Urban Growth in a Timely Manner," presented at the *4th International Conference on Integrating GIS and Environmental Modeling* (GIS/EM4), Banff, Alberta, Canada, 2000.

Clarke, Keith C., and Lenard Gaydos, "Loose-Coupling a Cellular Automaton Model and GIS: Long-Term Urban Growth Prediction for San Francisco and Washington/Baltimore," *International Journal of Geographical Information Systems*, Vol. 12, 1998, pp. 699–714.

Clarke, Keith C., Stacey Hoppen, and Lenard Gaydos, "A Self-Modifying Cellular Automaton Model of Historical Urbanization in the San Francisco Bay Area," *Environment and Planning B*, Vol. 24, 1997, pp. 247–261.

Collaborative Economics, *The Economic Future of the San Joaquin Valley*, The Great Valley Center, Modesto, California, 2000.

Dietzel, Charles K., "Spatio-Temporal Difference in Model Outputs and Parameter Space as Determined by Calibration Extent," in P. Atkinson, G. Foody, S. Darby, and F. Wu (eds), *Geodynamics*, CRC Press, Boca Raton, Florida, 2004.

Esnard, Ann-Margaret, and Yizhao Yang, "Descriptive and Comparative Studies of the 1990 Urban Extent Data for the New York Metropolitan Region," *URISA Journal*, Vol. 14, 2002, pp. 57–62.

Fulton, William, Madelyn Glickfeld, Grant McMurran, and June Gin, "A Landscape Portrait of Southern California's Structure of Government and Growth," Claremont Graduate University Research Institute, Claremont, California, July 1998.

Fulton, William, Rolf Pendall, Mai Nguyen, and Alicia Harrison, *Who Sprawls Most? How Growth Patterns Differ Across the U.S.*, The Brookings Institution, Washington, D.C., 2001.

Glickfeld, Madelyn, and Ned Levine, *Regional Growth . . . Local Reaction: The Enactment and Effects of Local Growth Control and Management Measures in California*, Lincoln Institute of Land Policy, Cambridge, Massachusetts, 1992.

Goldstein, Noah C., "Brains VS Braun—Comparative Strategies for the Calibration of a Cellular Automata-Based Urban Growth Model," in P. Atkinson, G. Foody, S. Darby, and F. Wu (eds), *Geodynamics*, CRC Press, Boca Raton, Florida, 2004.

Hollis, Linda, and William Fulton, "Open Space Protection: Conservation Meets Growth Management," Brookings Institution Center for Urban and Metropolitan Policy, Washington, D.C., 2002.

Jantz, Claire A., Scott J. Goetz, and Mary K. Shelley, "Using the SLEUTH Urban Growth Model to Simulate the Impacts of Future Policy Scenarios on Urban Land Use in the Baltimore/Washington Metropolitan Area," *Environment and Planning B*, Vol. 31, 2004, pp. 251–271.

Landis, John D., and Michael Reilly, "How We Will Grow: Baseline Projections of California's Urban Footprint through the Year 2100," University of California, Berkeley, Institute of Urban and Regional Development, IURD Working Paper Series, Paper WP-2003-04, August 1, 2003.

Lee, David R., and G. Thomas Sallee, "A Method of Measuring Shape," *The Geographical Review*, Vol. 60, 1970, pp. 555–563.

Lee, Ronald, Timothy Miller, and Ryan D. Edwards, *The Growth and Aging of California's Population: Demographic and Fiscal Projections, Characteristics and Service Needs*, California Policy Research Center, Berkeley, California (Center for the Economics and Demography of Aging, Institute of Business and Economic Research, University of California, Berkeley, 2003, CEDA Paper 2003-002CL), 2003

Lewis, Paul, *California's Housing Element Law: The Issue of Local Noncompliance,* Public Policy Institute of California, San Francisco, California, 2003.

McWilliams, Carey, *California: The Great Exception,* University of California Press, Berkeley, 1999. (Originally published 1949.)

Silva, Elizabete A., and Keith C. Clarke, "Calibration of the SLEUTH Urban Growth Model for Lisbon and Porto, Portugal," *Computers, Environment and Urban Systems,* Vol. 26, 2002, pp. 525–552.

Theobald, David M., "Land-Use Dynamics Beyond the Urban Fringe," *The Geographical Review,* Vol. 91, No. 3, 2001, pp. 544–564.

Weiser, Matt, "All Choked Up: Central California Finds One More Reason to Battle Sprawl," *Planning,* Vol. 70, No. 6, 2004, pp. 10–15.

Yang, Xiaojun, and C. P. Lo, "Modeling Urban Growth and Landscape Change in the Atlanta Metropolitan Area," *International Journal of Geographical Information Science,* Vol. 17, 2003, pp. 463–488.

About the Authors

MICHAEL B. TEITZ

Michael Teitz is a senior fellow at the Public Policy Institute of California and professor emeritus at the University of California, Berkeley, and the University of California, Merced. He is an expert on urban development and planning, regional and local economic development, and housing policy. He has served as an advisor to numerous government and private organizations, including the U.S. Department of Housing and Urban Development, the State of California, and the City of Los Angeles. He holds an M.S. in geography from the University of Wisconsin and a Ph.D. in regional science from the University of Pennsylvania.

CHARLES DIETZEL

Charles Dietzel is a dissertation fellow at the Public Policy Institute of California and a doctoral candidate in the Department of Geography at the University of California, Santa Barbara. His research interests include urban development and planning, spatial simulation and modeling, and geocomputation. He was the recipient of the UC Santa Barbara Department of Geography Excellence in Research Award, a National Science Foundation Dissertation Improvement Grant, and a University Consortium of GIS Student Paper Award. He holds an M.A. in landscape ecology from Duke University.

WILLIAM FULTON

William Fulton is president of Solimar Research Group in Ventura, California, and a senior scholar at the School of Planning, Policy, and Development at the University of Southern California. An expert on land-use and metropolitan growth policy, he is the author of four books, including *The Reluctant Metropolis: The Politics of Urban Growth in Los Angeles* and *Guide to California Planning*. He has also co-authored several seminal reports on emerging urban and regional growth issues. He holds an M.A. in urban planning from UCLA and an M.A. in mass communication from American University in Washington, D.C.

Related PPIC Publications

Metropolitan Growth Planning in California, 1900–2000
Elisa Barbour

The Central Valley at a Crossroads: Migration and Its Implications
Hans P. Johnson and Joseph M. Hayes

California's Housing Element Law: The Issue of Local Noncompliance.
Paul G. Lewis

"A State of Diversity: Demographic Trends in California's Regions"
California Counts: Population Trends and Profiles
Volume 3, Number 5, May 2002
Hans P. Johnson